Lozzy's Lenormand Card Combinations & Exercises

Lozzy Phillips

Lozzy's Lenormand Card Combinations & Exercises
by Lozzy Phillips

ISBN: 9781097101986

Published independently by Lozzy's Lenormand

www.lozzyslenormand.com

© 2019 Lozzy Phillips

All rights reserved. No portion of this book may be reproduced in any form without permission from the publisher, except as permitted by U.K. copyright law. For permissions contact:

lozzy@lozzyslenormand.com

CONTENTS

INTRODUCTION	7
ABOUT LENORMAND CARD COMBINATIONS	9
QUICK REFERENCE CARD MEANINGS	11
THE CARD COMBINATIONS	13
RIDER	15
CLOVER	17
SHIP	19
HOUSE	21
TREE	23
CLOUDS	25
SNAKE	27
COFFIN	29
BOUQUET	31
SCYTHE	33

WHIP	35
BIRDS	37
CHILD	39
FOX	41
BEAR	43
STARS	45
STORKS	47
DOG	49
TOWER	51
GARDEN	53
MOUNTAIN	55
CROSSROADS	57
MICE	59
HEART	61
RING	63
BOOK	65
LETTER	67

MAN	69
WOMAN	71
LILY	73
SUN	75
MOON	77
KEY	79
FISH	81
ANCHOR	83
CROSS	85
CARD MEANING & COMBO EXERCISES	87
ANSWERS	99
FINALLY!	107
ABOUT THE AUTHOR	109
OTHER BOOKS BY THIS AUTHOR	111

Introduction

I've long been a fan of fortune-telling cards.

My journey into cartomancy began many years ago using Tarot, but in recent years I found myself drawn to the more upfront, storytelling nature of the Lenormand, which doesn't have the mythic, subjective associations of the Tarot. I particularly like that with the Lenormand, what you see is what you get; the symbols are simple, universal and related to people's day to day lives. As more of an earthy than an esoteric person, this became a more appealing approach for me. With Lenormand, it's the particular card combinations that give the story of the reading – as well as the context in which the cards are read.

Like Tarot, Lenormand cards all have symbols; unlike the Tarot system, however, each card does not represent a particular stage on a journey, and there are no major and minor arcana. Lenormand symbols are very direct; a Key for the 'answer', for example, or a Book to represent 'knowledge'; a Ship is a journey of some kind, a Snake is a betrayal or problem. The Rider represents an arrival; the Sun, success.

There are various Lenormand decks; the traditional eighteenth century decks, usually with playing-card inserts, and countless more modern versions, many of which are beautiful 7and would be a positive addition to anybody's collection. The beauty of Lenormand, however, is that because the symbols are universal, anybody can make their own versions of the cards, which will have the added advantage of having a more personalised feel for them.

I've found the accuracy of readings with Lenormand cards to be quite startling at times, and thus have found them useful for guidance and support in all sorts of situations. I read the cards for myself and for others and I love experimenting with them. I've put this book together to help share all I've learned so far, and some techniques you can use to make the most of the cards yourself.

Happy reading!

About Lenormand Card Combinations

When I was first learning Lenormand, the hardest thing to remember was the card combinations. I used to go back, again and again, and spend time searching for lists and interpretations, desperately trying to memorise them all. And I know from my website that it is the card combination lists that my readers often head for first of all.

So as well as giving you those lists in a simple book-format, I wanted to help you go beyond that - and let you into a couple of the biggest secrets to understanding how to read Lenormand Card Combinations.

Secret #1

The combinations aren't particularly hard to learn as long as you know the meanings of each of the 36 cards. Some cards have more than one meaning, although you'll find these are also pretty logical. Once you've understood those meanings - and I mean, really understood them and thought in day to day terms about the symbols being used - the card combinations become relatively easy. As long as you know the second secret, which you'll find at the start of the Card Combinations chapter.

It's worth noting that the particular deck you use should NOT affect the meanings. The symbols of each card should mean the same things across all decks, regardless of any background images in that particular deck. You will find there are some minor differences in how individual readers interpret them, however. This can overcomplicate matters, especially for beginners. I'd try thinking instead about the different aspects of those real-life symbols for yourself. The Lenormand cards have a long history partly because the symbols used are universal, and speak to universal human concerns. Ask yourself :

- What does that object, or thing make me think of in real life?
- If it's an animal, what are the commonly known features of that animal?
- What aspects of our culture does each object, thing or animal bring to mind?
- What cultural and historical meanings and differences might there be in the meaning of that symbol?

Quick Reference Card Meanings

1. Rider		Arrival, New Situation or Individual, News; Upcoming
2. Clover		Luck, Opportunities, Chance
3. Ship		Journey, Travel, Transport, Movement
4. House		House, Home, Family, Family Name
5. Tree		Health, Healing, Spirituality, Growth
6. Clouds		Confusion, Uncertainty, Lack of Clarity
7. Snake		Betrayal, Big Problems, Untrustworthiness
8. Coffin		The End, Death, Ending, Finality
9. Bouquet		Loveliness, Beauty, Blessings, Gifts
10. Scythe		Cutting Out, Final Decision, Abrupt Ending, Surgery
11. Whip		A Hard Time, Abuse, Hard Work, Physical Activity, Sex
12. Birds		Conversation, Talk, Chatter, Discussion
13. Child		Child, Youngster, Beginner
14. Fox		Work, Survival, Cunning, Theft
15. Bear		Money, Finances; Power, Weight
16. Stars		Fame, Achievement, Goals, Famous or Admired Person

17. Storks	Fresh start, New Beginnings, Starting Again
18. Dog	Friendship, Friends, Allies, Soulmates, Faithfulness, Loyalty
19. Tower	Buildings, Corporations, Officialdom, Status, Height
20. Garden	Network, Marketplace, Group, Social Life, Public, Event
21. Mountain	Block, Rigidity, Delay, Obstacle
22. Crossroads	Options, Choices, Multiples, Fork in the Road
23. Mice	Worries, Anxiety, Troubles, Stress
24. Heart	Love, Passion, Love-Life, Caring, Core
25. Ring	Relationship, Contract, Payment, Marriage, Bond
26. Book	Knowledge, Learning, Secrets, Study
27. Letter	Letter, News, Message, Written Document
28. Man	Man, The Questioner, Male, Masculine
29. Woman	Woman, The Questioner, Female, Feminine
30. Lily	Age, Older person, Retirement, Later Life, Maturity
31. Sun	Success, Happiness, Joy, Sunshine
32. Moon	Emotions, Creativity, Feelings
33. Key	Destiny, Fate, Significance, Importance, Karma
34. Fish	Business, Freelancing, Independence, Cashflow
35. Anchor	Stability, The Long Term, Permanence
36. Cross	Burden, Worries, Depression, Religion, Negativity

The Card Combinations

Secret #2

To 'get' card combinations, the next thing is to know **how the cards work together in pairs**.

The first card in the pair can be read as a **Noun** - a thing, a person, a name

The second card in the pair can be read as an **Adjective** - the *description* of that thing or person

e.g. **Sun** + **Mountain** = Success (Noun) + Blocked/Delayed (Adjective)
= Blocked/Delayed Success
Man + **Bouqu**et = Man (Noun) + Pleasant/Good-looking (Adjective)
= Pleasant or Good-looking Man

When you read through these combination lists, bear this in mind to see how I've come up with the meaning I have. And when you read through other people's lists in future, you should be able to do the same. Although it might seem on the surface as if our interpretations are wildly different, once you start getting your head around the cards and how combinations work, you should be able to see those fundamental meanings underneath. Sometimes you'll find you do have to use a bit of intuition, your knowledge of the world, and some lateral thinking to find a realistic meaning for a particular combination.

In addition to exercises to test the card meanings, I've also provided some card combination exercises at the end of the book to give you some extra practice in thinking this way.

Exercises 5 & 6 in particular should give you some great practice in this. I hope you find them useful.

1. RIDER

Rider & Clover	Chance arrival or encounter; luck on the way
Rider & Ship	Overseas visitor or news, fleeting encounter, delivery
Rider & House	House or family news; house guest; visitor; new house
Rider & Tree	Spiritual encounter, improved health upcoming
Rider & Clouds	Confusing news or message; upcoming uncertainty
Rider & Snake	Difficult news; oncoming challenges; problems ahead
Rider & Coffin	Big changes, period of transition, mourning; final visit
Rider & Bouquet	Good things ahead, happy news, gift delivery
Rider & Scythe	Separation, sudden decision, accident news
Rider & Whip	Sexual encounter; argument; hard times coming
Rider & Birds	Announcements; news; phone calls
Rider & Child	Pregnancy news; birth announcements
Rider & Fox	Job news; new employee
Rider & Bear	Money arriving; financial news
Rider & Stars	Achievement news; hope; assistance
Rider & Storks	Fresh start coming; changes ahead

Rider & Dog	friend's news; friend visiting
Rider & Tower	business acquisition; official status coming
Rider & Garden	networking; upcoming socialising; guests
Rider & Mountain	delays ahead; slowing down
Rider & Crossroad	choices ahead; new possibilities
Rider & Mice	worrying news; stressful times
Rider & Heart	new lover; greater intimacy
Rider & Ring	commitment; proposal; new contract; marriage
Rider & Book	discovery; lesson; new project
Rider & Letter	news; message; mail; documents; delivery
Rider & Man	new man in your life; man's news; male visitor
Rider & Woman	new woman in your life; woman's news; female visitor
Rider & Lily	ageing; arrival of wisdom; pending retirement
Rider & Sun	success is coming; victory; achievement
Rider & Moon	new romance; upcoming creative period; rush of emotions
Rider & Key	significant event coming; spiritual lesson; turning point
Rider & Fish	new business; independence coming
Rider & Anchor	about to settle down; stability coming; reassurance
Rider & Cross	painful times; concerns ahead

2. CLOVER

Clover & Rider	upcoming opportunity; luck or a win on the way
Clover & Ship	overseas opportunity; last-minute travel; happy trip
Clover & House	prosperous family; happy home
Clover & Tree	recovery; great health; spiritual protection
Clover & Clouds.	dodgy opportunities; gambling addiction; foolishness
Clover & Snake	opportunist; gambler; false opportunity
Clover & Coffin.	risky situation; misfortune; luck ends; unlucky outcome
Clover & Bouquet	good luck; happiness; lovely surprise;
Clover & Scythe	stroke of luck; sudden opportunity
Clover & Whip	hard work brings luck; hard-won victory;
Clover & Birds	lucky conversations; lucky partnerships
Clover & Child	beginner's luck; surprise pregnancy; happy child
Clover & Fox	job or career opportunity; promotion; luck at work
Clover & Bear	unexpected windfall; win; financial opportunity
Clover & Stars	very good luck; surprise fame; lucky chances
Clover & Storks	positive change; new start improves things

CLOVER & DOG	FRIEND'S LUCK; POSITIVE INFLUENCES; GOOD FRIENDSHIPS
CLOVER & TOWER	STATUS LUCK; CASINOS; HIGH STATUS OPPORTUNITIES
CLOVER & GARDEN	LOTTERY; GAMES; PUBLIC OPPORTUNITY
CLOVER & MOUNTAIN	RETREAT; HOLIDAY; BLOCKED OPPORTUNITIES
CLOVER & CROSSROAD	MULTIPLE OPPORTUNITIES; BREAKTHROUGH;
CLOVER & MICE	NERVOUS ANTICIPATION, BUTTERFLIES; GAMBLING WORRIES
CLOVER & HEART	LOVE OPPORTUNITY; IN LOVE; LUCKY LOVE RELATIONSHIP
CLOVER & RING	LUCKY ASSOCIATION OR CONTRACT; HAPPY MARRIAGE
CLOVER & BOOK	REVELATIONS, DISCOVERIES; LEARNING OPPORTUNITY;
CLOVER & LETTER	LUCKY NEWS; WIN OR OFFER NOTIFICATION; LOTTERY TICKET
CLOVER & MAN	LUCKY MAN; OPPORTUNIST; POSITIVE THINKER; RISK TAKER
CLOVER & WOMAN	LUCKY WOMAN; OPPORTUNIST; RISK TAKER
CLOVER & LILY	LUCK BORNE OUT OF EXPERIENCE; HAPPY RETIREMENT
CLOVER & SUN	OVERNIGHT SUCCESS; AMAZING ACHIEVEMENT
CLOVER & MOON	CREATIVE OR ROMANTIC OPPORTUNITIES; ROMANTIC LUCK
CLOVER & KEY	LUCKY BREAK; POSITIVE TWIST OF FATE;
CLOVER & FISH	BUSINESS OPPORTUNITY; PROSPERITY, FINANCIAL LUCK
CLOVER & ANCHOR	LONG-TERM PROSPERITY; ALWAYS FALLING ON FEET
CLOVER & CROSS	THINGS WORK OUT IN THE END; SILVER LINING

3. SHIP

SHIP & RIDER	RETURN; ROUND TRIP; UPCOMING JOURNEY
SHIP & CLOVER	LUCKY JOURNEY; ENTERTAINING TRIP
SHIP & HOUSE	HOUSEBOAT; IMMIGRATION/EMIGRATION; MOVING AWAY
SHIP & TREE	SPIRITUAL JOURNEY; HEALTH-RELATED TRIP; SPA HOLIDAY
SHIP & CLOUDS	TRANSIENCE; ADVENTURE; UNCERTAIN JOURNEY
SHIP & SNAKE	DIFFICULT TRIP; BUMPY RIDE; TRAVEL PROBLEMS
SHIP & COFFIN	JOURNEY'S END; CANCELLED TRIP; FINAL JOURNEY
SHIP & BOUQUET	PLEASANT TRIP; LUXURY TRAVEL; CRUISE
SHIP & SCYTHE	TRIP CUT SHORT; LAST-MINUTE CANCELLATION; ACCIDENT
SHIP & WHIP	ROUGH JOURNEY; SPORTS TRIP; SEXUAL JOURNEY
SHIP & BIRDS	FOREIGN LANGUAGE; PLANE; PASSENGERS; TOURISTS
SHIP & CHILD	PREGNANCY KID'S TRIP; BEGINNER'S JOURNEY
SHIP & FOX	WORK TRAVEL; TRAVEL EMPLOYEE; STOWAWAY
SHIP & BEAR	MONEY TRANSFER; OVERSEAS MONEY; POWER HANDOVER
SHIP & STARS	SPACE EXPLORATION, ROCKET; FLYING; JOURNEY TO FAME
SHIP & STORKS	MOVING ON; START OF A NEW JOURNEY

SHIP & DOG	INTERNATIONAL FRIENDS; TRAVEL COMPANION
SHIP & TOWER	OFFICIAL TRIP; FOREIGN COMPANY OR GOVERNMENT
SHIP & GARDEN	GROUP TRIP; WORLD TRAVEL; FOREIGN COUNTRIES
SHIP & MOUNTAIN	DELAYED TRIP; BLOCKED JOURNEY; BORDERS
SHIP & CROSSROAD	MULTIPLE TRIPS; CHOICE OF ROUTE; EXCURSIONS
SHIP & MICE	STRESSFUL TRIP; ANXIOUS JOURNEY
SHIP & HEART	ROMANTIC TRIP; HOLIDAY ROMANCE; OVERSEAS LOVE
SHIP & RING	HONEYMOON; OVERSEAS WEDDING; FOREIGN CONTRACT
SHIP & BOOK	RESEARCH; JOURNEY TO PUBLICATION; EDUCATIONAL TRIP
SHIP & LETTER	TRAVEL DOCUMENTS; OVERSEAS NEWS; LETTER IN TRANSIT
SHIP & MAN	MALE TRAVELER; FOREIGNER
SHIP & WOMAN.	FEMALE TRAVELER; FOREIGNER
SHIP & LILY	EXTENDED TRIP; OLDER TRAVELLER
SHIP & SUN	SUCCESSFUL JOURNEY; HOT COUNTRY; SUMMER HOLIDAY
SHIP & MOON	DAY-DREAMS; CREATIVE JOURNEY; OVERNIGHT TRAVEL; MOOD SWINGS
SHIP & KEY	SIGNIFICANT JOURNEY; KARMA; TRIP OF A LIFETIME
SHIP & FISH	BUSINESS TRIP; TRANSPORTATION; TRADE
SHIP & ANCHOR	NEVER-ENDING JOURNEY; LONG TRIP; ARRIVAL
SHIP & CROSS	PILGRIMAGE, RELIGIOUS JOURNEY; PROBLEMATIC TRIP

4. HOUSE

HOUSE & RIDER	VISIT; GUEST; GUESTHOUSE
HOUSE & CLOVER	FORTUNATE FAMILY; GOOD LOCATION; NICE PLACE
HOUSE & SHIP	MOVING HOUSE; MOVING AWAY; HOUSEBOAT; CAMPER VAN
HOUSE & TREE	HEALTH CENTRE; SPIRITUAL HOME; KARMIC FAMILY
HOUSE & CLOUDS	DOMESTIC ISSUES; PROBLEMS AT HOME
HOUSE & SNAKE	ABUSIVE HOME OR FAMILY; DOMESTIC ARGUMENTS
HOUSE & COFFIN	FAMILY DEATH; HOUSE SALE
HOUSE & BOUQUET	LOVELY HOME; INTERIOR DESIGN; PLEASANT FAMILY
HOUSE & SCYTHE	SEPARATION, FAMILY SPLIT; SUDDEN HOUSE SALE
HOUSE & WHIP	DOMESTIC QUARRELS; GYM; BORDELLO
HOUSE & BIRDS	DOMESTIC PARTNERS; HOUSEMATES; MEETING-HOUSE
HOUSE & CHILD	CHILDHOOD HOME; STARTER HOME; SMALL HOUSE
HOUSE & FOX	BUILDER; HOMEWORKER; DOMESTIC EMPLOYEE; AGENCY
HOUSE & BEAR	BUY-TO-LET; WEALTHY OR POWERFUL FAMILY
HOUSE & STARS	DREAM HOUSE; CELEBRITY HOME; FAMOUS FAMILY
HOUSE & STORKS	NEW HOME; MOVING HOUSE; HOUSE EXTENSION

HOUSE & DOG	PETS; FRIENDLY FAMILY; FRIEND'S HOUSE; HOUSEMATES
HOUSE & TOWER	FLATS, TOWER BLOCK; HOUSING ASSOC; ESTATE AGENCY
HOUSE & GARDEN	BIG FAMILY; STATELY HOME; PUB, CAFE; THEATRE
HOUSE & MOUNTAIN	BLOCKED HOUSE-SALE; CHALET; REMOTE LOCATION
HOUSE & CROSSROAD	MULTIPLE HOMES; CHOICE OF HOUSES
HOUSE & MICE	DOMESTIC WORRIES; ANXIOUS MOVE; WORRIED FAMILY
HOUSE & HEART	LOVING HOME; FAMILY; HEARTH & HOME
HOUSE & RING	LEASE OR CONTRACT SIGNED; FAMILY NAME; HOUSEHOLD
HOUSE & BOOK	PUBLISHING HOUSE; SECRET ROOMS; FAMILY SECRET; LIBRARY
HOUSE & LETTER	HOUSE DOCUMENTS; DEEDS; FAMILY DOCUMENTS
HOUSE & MAN	HOMEOWNER; LANDLORD; MAN'S HOME
HOUSE & WOMAN	HOMEOWNER; LANDLADY; WOMAN'S HOME
HOUSE & LILY	OLD HOUSE; ESTABLISHED FAMILY
HOUSE & SUN	SUCCESS AT HOME; HIGH-ACHIEVING FAMILY
HOUSE & MOON	FANTASY HOME; CREATIVE PLACE; EMOTIONAL FAMILY
HOUSE & KEY	IMPORTANT HOUSE; SPIRITUAL HOMECOMING
HOUSE & FISH	HOME-BASED BUSINESS; ESTATE AGENT; BRAND
HOUSE & ANCHOR	LONG-TERM SECURITY; COMMITTED FAMILY
HOUSE & CROSS	CHURCH; HOUSE WITH NEGATIVE HISTORY

5. TREE

TREE & RIDER:	GOOD HEALTH ON ITS WAY; HEALTH NEWS; KARMA
TREE & CLOVER:	LUCKY KARMA; GOOD HEALTH; FORTUNATE DEVELOPMENT
TREE & SHIP:	HEALTH-RELATED TRIP; SPIRITUAL JOURNEY
TREE & HOUSE:	FAMILY HEALTH; HEALTH SPA; STRUCTURAL HEALTH
TREE & CLOUDS:	UNDER THE WEATHER; MYSTERY AILMENT; HEALTH ISSUE
TREE & SNAKE:	SICKNESS, BUG; STOMACH PROBLEM; SEXUAL FUNCTION
TREE & COFFIN:	SERIOUS ILLNESS; DECLINING HEALTH; DEPRESSION
TREE & BOUQUET:	FLOURISHING; HEALTH & WELLBEING; IMPROVEMENTS
TREE & SCYTHE:	SUDDEN ILLNESS; SURGERY; REDUCED VITALITY
TREE & WHIP:	SEXUAL HEALTH; SPORTS INJURY; MUSCLE STRAIN
TREE & BIRDS:	THERAPY; VOICE PROBLEMS; VOCAL HEALTH
TREE & CHILD:	PREGNANCY; CHILDHOOD ILLNESS; SMALL HEALTH ISSUE
TREE & FOX:	UNDISCOVERED HEALTH PROBLEM; OCCUPATIONAL HEALTH
TREE & BEAR:	WEIGHT ISSUES; DIETARY HEALTH; FINANCIAL HEALTH OR GROWTH
TREE & STARS:	RECOVERY; EXCELLENT HEALTH; HEALING; HEALTH GOALS
TREE & STORKS:	BOUNCING BACK; NEW LEASE OF LIFE; NEW LIFESTYLE; BIRTH

TREE & DOG:	SOULMATE; DEEP FRIENDSHIP; HOLISTIC HEALTH
TREE & TOWER:	HOSPITAL, CLINIC, HEALTH CENTRE; ORGANISATIONAL HEALTH
TREE & GARDEN:	SPA; PUBLIC HEALTH; OUTDOOR ACTIVITIES
TREE & MOUNTAIN:	BLOCKAGE; EXHAUSTION, FEELING SLUGGISH
TREE & CROSSROAD:	DIFFERENT TREATMENT OPTIONS; SPIRITUAL CHOICES
TREE & MICE:	STRESS, ANXIETY; HEALTH WORRIES; HYPOCHONDRIA
TREE & HEART	HEART TROUBLE; RELATIONSHIP HEALTH; OLD LOVE
TREE & RING	MARRIAGE HEALTH: KARMIC BOND: RECURRING HEALTH ISSUE
TREE & BOOK;	CHECK-UP; HIDDEN HEALTH ISSUE; RESEARCHING SYMPTOMS
TREE & LETTER;	HEALTH CERTIFICATE; DOCTOR'S NOTE; PRESCRIPTION
TREE & MAN:	MAN'S HEALTH; HEALER; PAST LIFE CONNECTION
TREE & WOMAN:	WOMAN'S HEALTH; HEALER, PAST LIFE CONNECTION
TREE & LILY:	AGEING HEALTH ISSUES; HEALTH IN SENIOR YEARS
TREE & SUN:	EXCELLENT HEALTH; RECOVERY; SUN-SCREEN
TREE & MOON:	EMOTIONAL HEALTH; HORMONE ISSUES
TREE & KEY:	KARMA; LIFE PURPOSE; LIFE LESSON; VITALITY
TREE & FISH:	FERTILITY; LIVING UNASSISTED; BUSINESS HEALTH
TREE & ANCHOR:	LONG-TERM HEALTH AND WELLBEING; LASTING VITALITY
TREE & CROSS:	DEPRESSION; CHRONIC HEALTH ISSUES

6. CLOUDS

Clouds & Rider: CONFUSING TIMES COMING; UNCLEAR MESSAGE

Clouds & Clover: HAPPY OBLIVION; STUMBLING INTO LUCKY CIRCUMSTANCES

Clouds & Ship: UNCERTAIN OR UNCLEAR JOURNEY

Clouds & House;   UNCERTAIN LIVING CIRCUMSTANCES; HOUSE SALE PROBLEMS

Clouds & Tree: VAGUE SYMPTOMS; HEALTH UNCERTAINTY: MENTAL HEALTH

Clouds & Snake: COMPLICATIONS; SNAKE OIL; DELIBERATE CONFUSION

Clouds & Coffin: CLARITY; RESOLUTION; PROBLEMS END; GRIEF SYMPTOMS

Clouds & Bouquet: DREAMS; DAYDREAMS; HAPPILY TIPSY

Clouds & Scythe: CUT THROUGH CONFUSION; SHARPNESS; BAD DECISIONS

Clouds & Whip: GASLIGHTING; ABUSE; BLURRING OF SEXUAL BOUNDARIES

Clouds & Birds: MISCOMMUNICATION; MISUNDERSTANDING; RUMOUR

Clouds & Child: CHILDLIKE CONFUSION; SMALL MISUNDERSTANDING

Clouds & Fox   CORRUPTION; MANIPULATION; JOB UNCERTAINTY

Clouds & Bear: MONEY ISSUES; POOR MANAGER; UNCERTAIN FINANCES

Clouds & Stars: FANTASIES; LAZINESS; DELUSIONS OF GRANDEUR

Clouds & Storks: STEP INTO THE UNKNOWN; UNCERTAIN CHANGE

CLOUDS & DOG:	DISLOYALTY; UNTRUSTWORTHY FRIEND; BETRAYAL
CLOUDS & TOWER:	SHADY CORPORATION; MURKY OFFICIALDOM; COVERUP
CLOUDS & GARDEN:	EVENT MARRED; NETWORKING ISSUES
CLOUDS & MOUNTAIN:	WARNING; RED FLAGS; DELAYS AND CONFUSION
CLOUDS & CROSSROAD:	CHOICES OBSCURED; PATH UNCERTAIN
CLOUDS & MICE:	ANXIOUS CONFUSION; WORRIES; DEMENTIA; FEAR
CLOUDS & HEART:	CHEATING; UNCERTAIN ROMANCE
CLOUDS & RING:	MARRIAGE PROBLEMS; HIDDEN MARRIAGE; DODGY DEAL
CLOUDS & BOOK:	SECRETS; HIDDEN KNOWLEDGE; PLAGIARISM
CLOUDS & LETTER:	FORGERY; FAKE NEWS; LACK OF WRITTEN CLARITY
CLOUDS & MAN:	CONMAN; UNSTABLE MAN; MAN'S UNCERTAINTY
CLOUDS & WOMAN:	CON-WOMAN; UNSTABLE WOMAN; WOMAN'S UNCERTAINTY
CLOUDS & LILY:	DEMENTIA; MEMORY PROBLEMS; OLD AGE FORGETFULNESS
CLOUDS & SUN:	VICTORY IN THE END; ALL COMES GOOD
CLOUDS & MOON:	EMOTIONAL CONFUSION; MOODINESS
CLOUDS & KEY:	RESOLUTION; THE ANSWER IS FOUND
CLOUDS & FISH:	DODGY BUSINESS PRACTICES; BUSINESS UNCERTAINTY
CLOUDS & ANCHOR:	LONG-TERM UNCERTAINTY; STABILITY IN CONFUSION
CLOUDS & CROSS:	DESPAIR, HOPELESSNESS; DEMENTIA

7. SNAKE

SNAKE & RIDER:	HELP COMING; DISHONEST NEWS; LIES
SNAKE & CLOVER:	SOLUTION; REPAIRS; LUCKY WOMAN
SNAKE & SHIP:	TRAVEL PROBLEMS; TRIP WITH A LIAR
SNAKE & HOUSE:	UNTRUSTWORTHY FAMILY; DOMESTIC PROBLEMS
SNAKE & TREE:	HEALTH PROBLEMS; HEALTHY CYNICISM
SNAKE & CLOUDS:	CONFUSION; GASLIGHTING; NO SOLUTION
SNAKE & COFFIN:	PROBLEMS ENDING; TERMINAL PROBLEM
SNAKE & BOUQUET:	POSITIVE RESOLUTION; SILVER LINING
SNAKE & SCYTHE:	SURGERY, RECOVERY; SWIFT REMOVAL OF PROBLEM
SNAKE & WHIP:	ABUSE, SEXUAL ABUSE; INJURY; PROMISCUITY
SNAKE & BIRDS:	NEGATIVE GOSSIP, SLANDER; DIFFICULT NEGOTIATIONS
SNAKE & CHILD:	DIFFICULT OR PROBLEM CHILD; CHILDISH BETRAYER
SNAKE & FOX:	WORK PROBLEMS; UNTRUSTWORTHY EMPLOYEE; WORK RIVAL
SNAKE & BEAR:	MONEY TROUBLES; BAD MANAGER; CONTROL FREAK
SNAKE & STARS:	DIFFICULT PROJECT; CHALLENGING HIGH-FLYER;
SNAKE & STORKS:	RISKY MOVE; DIFFICULT NEW START; FALSE START

SNAKE & DOG:	UNTRUSTWORTHY FRIEND; WRONG ADVICE
SNAKE & TOWER:	HIGH-LEVEL CORRUPTION; LAWSUIT
SNAKE & GARDEN:	UNTRUSTWORTHY SOCIAL CONNECTION; DIFFICULT EVENT
SNAKE & MOUNTAIN:	BIG BLOCKS; UNRESOLVED TROUBLES; TROUBLES PREVENTED
SNAKE & CROSSROAD:	MULTIPLE DECEPTIONS; RUNNING AWAY FROM PROBLEMS
SNAKE & MICE:	MAJOR PROBLEMS; ANXIETY; THINGS GET WORSE
SNAKE & HEART:	ROMANTIC BETRAYAL; CHEATING; SEDUCTION
SNAKE & RING:	BROKEN CONTRACT; RELATIONSHIP PROBLEMS; BAD DEAL
SNAKE & BOOK:	SECRET BETRAYAL; HIDDEN PROBLEMS; UNPLEASANT SECRETS
SNAKE & LETTER:	BAD NEWS; NEGATIVE REVIEW; FAKE NEWS
SNAKE & MAN:	CONMAN; CHEATING MAN; UNTRUSTWORTHY MAN
SNAKE & WOMAN:	FEMALE CON ARTIST; CHEAT; UNTRUSTWORTHY WOMAN
SNAKE & LILY:	CHEATING OLDER MAN; AGEING PROBLEMS
SNAKE & SUN:	SUCCESS AFTER DIFFICULTIES; COSTLY SUCCESS
SNAKE & MOON:	EMOTIONAL PROBLEMS; BAD MOODS; ILLUSIONS
SNAKE & KEY:	SOLUTION; SUCCESS AFTER BETRAYAL; DODGING A BULLET
SNAKE & FISH:	BUSINESS TROUBLES; FRAUD; THREAT TO INDEPENDENCE
SNAKE & ANCHOR:	LONG-TERM PROBLEMS; INSECURITY; INSTABILITY
SNAKE & CROSS:	BIG PROBLEMS; SUFFERING; BETRAYAL; GUILT

8. COFFIN

COFFIN & RIDER:	ENDING, BIG CHANGE COMING
COFFIN & CLOVER:	LUCKY ENDING; SECOND CHANCE
COFFIN & SHIP:	MOVING AWAY; EMIGRATION; DEATH
COFFIN & HOUSE:	HOUSE MOVE; RESTRUCTURE; FAMILY TOMB
COFFIN & TREE:	ILLNESS; DEPRESSION; SPIRITUAL ENDING
COFFIN & CLOUDS:	MENTAL ILLNESS; NERVOUS BREAKDOWN
COFFIN & SNAKE:	BIG PROBLEMS; DIFFICULT ENDING
COFFIN & BOUQUET:	RECOVERY; FUNERAL; HAPPY ENDING
COFFIN & SCYTHE:	ACCIDENT; TROUBLES END; BAD DECISIONS
COFFIN & WHIP:	ABUSE; VIOLENCE; DESTRUCTION
COFFIN & BIRDS:	COMMUNICATION ENDS; NEGATIVE CONVERSATION
COFFIN & CHILD:	DESTRUCTIVE CHILD; NEW START AFTER PROBLEMS
COFFIN & FOX:	JOB LOSS; DECEIT ENDS
COFFIN & BEAR:	INHERITANCE; FINANCIAL CHANGES
COFFIN & STARS:	HOPE; RELIEF; IMPROVEMENTS; POSITIVE ENDING
COFFIN & STORKS:	LETTING GO; NEGATIVE CHANGE

COFFIN & DOG:	FRIEND IN NEED; FRIENDSHIP ENDS
COFFIN & TOWER:	CORPORATE END; OFFICIAL ENDING; PRISON; MORGUE
COFFIN & GARDEN:	FUNERAL; CEMETERY; CANCELLED EVENT
COFFIN & MOUNTAIN:	STUCK; ISOLATION; LACK OF MOVEMENT
COFFIN & CROSSROAD:	NEW DIRECTION; CHOICE OF ENDINGS
COFFIN & MICE:	FEARS, WORRIES; ANXIOUS DEPRESSION
COFFIN & HEART:	GRIEF; HEARTACHE; END OF ROMANCE
COFFIN & RING:	MARRIAGE ENDING; RELATIONSHIP OVER; CONTRACT ENDS
COFFIN & BOOK:	SECRET REVEALED; AUTOPSY
COFFIN & LETTER:	OBITUARY; WILL; RESIGNATION LETTER; CANCELLATION
COFFIN & MAN:	ILL OR DEPRESSED MAN; MALE ENDING
COFFIN & WOMAN:	ILL OR DEPRESSED WOMAN; FEMALE ENDING
COFFIN & LILY:	OLD AGE; DYING;; MATURE ENDING
COFFIN & SUN:	SECOND CHANCE; SUCCESS IN THE END
COFFIN & MOON:	SHOCK; EMOTIONAL ENDING; GRIEF
COFFIN & KEY:	KARMA; A LIFE-CHANGER; NECESSARY ENDING
COFFIN & FISH:	FUNERAL BUSINESS; BUSINESS FAILURE; LOSS OF MONEY
COFFIN & ANCHOR:	LONG-TERM TROUBLES; LONGING
COFFIN & CROSS:	PAIN; GRIEF; SERIOUS DEPRESSION

9. BOUQUET

BOUQUET & RIDER:	GIFT; PLEASANT VISITOR; POSITIVE ENCOUNTER
BOUQUET & CLOVER:	JOY; GOOD LUCK; SURPRISE GIFT
BOUQUET & SHIP:	PLEASANT TRIP; LOVELY HOLIDAY
BOUQUET & HOUSE:	HOME DECORATING; BEAUTIFUL HOUSE; PLEASANT HOME;
BOUQUET & TREE:	BLOOMING HEALTH; NATURE
BOUQUET & CLOUDS:	DAYDREAMS; PLEASANT FANTASIES; LAZINESS
BOUQUET & SNAKE:	TEMPTING BEAUTY; ALL THAT GLITTERS; JEALOUSY
BOUQUET & COFFIN:	FUNERAL FLOWERS; DISAPPOINTMENT, LET-DOWN
BOUQUET & SCYTHE:	PLASTIC SURGERY; POSITIVE DECISION
BOUQUET & WHIP:	SEXUAL PLEASURE; ENDORPHINS; DANCING
BOUQUET & BIRDS:	PLEASANT CONVERSATION; GOOD-LOOKING COUPLE
BOUQUET & CHILD:	CHILDLIKE PLEASURE; SMALL PLEASURES; ATTRACTIVE CHILD
BOUQUET & FOX:	WORK GIFT; BEAUTY JOB; FLORIST; FEIGNED POSITIVITY
BOUQUET & BEAR:	FINANCIAL GIFT; GOOD FINANCIAL SITUATION
BOUQUET & STARS:	ACCOLADE, RECOGNITION; DREAMS COME TRUE
BOUQUET & STORKS:	POSITIVE NEW BEGINNING; HAPPY ARRIVAL; PROGRESS

BOUQUET & DOG:	GOOD FRIENDSHIP; LOVELY FRIEND
BOUQUET & TOWER:	BEAUTY AND FASHION INDUSTRY; SHOPPING MALL
BOUQUET & GARDEN:	PARTY; GARDEN; HAPPY EVENT; PARK; LANDSCAPE
BOUQUET & MOUNTAIN:	DELAYED PLEASURE; HIKING; OUTDOORS
BOUQUET & CROSSROAD:	POSITIVE OPPORTUNITIES; MULTIPLE BLESSINGS
BOUQUET & MICE:	BUTTERFLIES; ANTICIPATION; HAPPINESS SHORT-LIVED
BOUQUET & HEART:	LOVE BLESSING; POSITIVE LOVE RELATIONSHIP
BOUQUET & RING:	GOOD CONTRACT; HAPPY MARRIAGE
BOUQUET & BOOK:	SECRET GIFT; LEARNING SOMETHING PLEASANT; BOOK PRIZE
BOUQUET & LETTER:	GIFT DELIVERY; GOOD NEWS; INVITATION
BOUQUET & MAN:	MALE CHARM; HANDSOME; GENTLEMAN
BOUQUET & WOMAN:	FEMALE CHARM; BEAUTY; LADYLIKE
BOUQUET & LILY:	SERENITY; PEACE; WISDOM; ACCEPTANCE; BLESSINGS OF EXPERIENCE
BOUQUET & SUN:	GREAT SUCCESS; WIN; CELEBRATION
BOUQUET & MOON:	ROMANTIC HAPPINESS; CREATIVE BLOSSOMING; FULFILMENT
BOUQUET & KEY:	SIGNIFICANT BLESSING; GREAT SUCCESS; VERY BEAUTIFUL
BOUQUET & FISH:	THRIVING BUSINESS; BEAUTY INDUSTRY
BOUQUET & ANCHOR:	LONG TERM POSITIVITY; HAPPINESS; GOALS REACHED
BOUQUET & CROSS:	CHARITY; BURDENED HAPPINESS; LOADED GIFT

10. SCYTHE

SCYTHE & RIDER:	SUDDEN DECISION; UNEXPECTED NEWS
SCYTHE & CLOVER:	LUCKY DECISION; GOOD RESULTS
SCYTHE & SHIP:	JOURNEY ABRUPTLY ENDED; ACCIDENT; TRIP CUT SHORT
SCYTHE & HOUSE:	DECISION ABOUT HOUSE; DAMAGED HOME; HOMELESS
SCYTHE & TREE:	SURGERY; HEALTH DECISION; TREE FELLED
SCYTHE & CLOUDS:	INDECISION; BAD DECISION; UNCLEAR OUTCOME
SCYTHE & SNAKE:	BAD DECISION; ATTACK PHYSICAL HARM
SCYTHE & COFFIN:	FINALITY, FINAL DECISION; VIOLENCE; HARM
SCYTHE & BOUQUET:	POSITIVE DECISION; PROBLEMS RESOLVED
SCYTHE & WHIP:	TOUGH DECISION; ELIMINATION ROUND; WEAPONS
SCYTHE & BIRDS:	BREAK-UP; VERBAL BREVITY; ARGUMENTS; VICIOUSNESS
SCYTHE & CHILD:	CHILDHOOD ACCIDENT; GROWING UP SUDDENLY
SCYTHE & FOX:	JOB CUTS; JOB LOSS; WORK DECISION
SCYTHE & BEAR:	FINANCIAL LOSSES; POWER REMOVED; DIET
SCYTHE & STARS:	CUT DOWN TO SIZE; DIMINISHED; POSITIVE DECISION
SCYTHE & STORKS:	MOVING ON QUICKLY; FALSE START

SCYTHE & DOG:	EXILE; END OF FRIENDSHIP; LETTING GO
SCYTHE & TOWER:	EMERGENCY ROOM; FALL OF OFFICIAL BODY; GOVT CUTS
SCYTHE & GARDEN:	ISOLATED, OSTRACISED: GARDENING: CANCELLATION
SCYTHE & MOUNTAIN:	DECISION DELAYED OR BLOCKED; INCOMPLETE
SCYTHE & CROSSROAD:	MULTIPLE CHOICES; FINAL DECISION; SUDDEN DECISION
SCYTHE & MICE:	STRESSFUL DECISION; POOR CHOICE
SCYTHE & HEART:	LOVE SPLIT; HEARTBREAK; RELATIONSHIP DECISION
SCYTHE & RING:	DIVORCE; SEPARATION; BROKEN AGREEMENT; CUT TIES
SCYTHE & BOOK:	SECRET UNCOVERED; DISCOVERY
SCYTHE & LETTER:	CENSORSHIP; EDITING; DIVORCE PAPERS; HURTFUL NEWS
SCYTHE & MAN:	DECISIVE MAN; SURGEON; JUDGMENTAL MAN
SCYTHE & WOMAN:	DECISIVE WOMAN; SURGEON; JUDGMENTAL WOMAN
SCYTHE & LILY:	SUDDEN RETIREMENT; MATURE DECISION
SCYTHE & SUN:	SUCCESSFUL DECISION; GOOD RESULTS
SCYTHE & MOON:	ROMANTIC SPLIT; CREATIVE DECISION; SUDDEN INSIGHT
SCYTHE & KEY:	DECISIVE MOMENT; KEY TURNING-POINT; FATE
SCYTHE & FISH:	BUSINESS DECISION; FINANCIAL DECISION
SCYTHE & ANCHOR:	LONG TERM DECISION; NO TURNING BACK
SCYTHE & CROSS:	PAINFUL DECISION; SUFFERING; SELF-HARM

11. WHIP

WHIP & RIDER:	HARSH FEEDBACK; ABUSE; REVENGE; CRITICISM
WHIP & CLOVER:	GOOD SEX; HARD WORK GETS RESULTS; GAMBLING
WHIP & SHIP	BUMPY RIDE; DIFFICULT JOURNEY; SPORTS TRIP
WHIP & HOUSE:	DOMESTIC ABUSE; HOME GYM
WHIP & TREE:	HEALTH PROBLEMS; NEGATIVE KARMA; INJURY
WHIP & CLOUDS:	PSYCHOLOGICAL ABUSE; DEMENTIA; CONFUSED SEXUALITY;
WHIP & SNAKE:	TROUBLEMAKER; FEMALE SEXUALITY; DANGER
WHIP & COFFIN:	SERIOUS HARM; END OF ABUSE; DESTRUCTION
WHIP & BOUQUET:	PLEASURABLE SEX; EXERCISE HIGH
WHIP & SCYTHE:	VIOLENCE; B.D.S.M; ACCIDENT
WHIP & BIRDS:	PHONE SEX; TOUGH DEBATE; VERBAL ABUSE; ARGUMENT
WHIP & CHILD:	TRAINING, COACHING, KIDS' SPORTS; ACTIVE CHILD
WHIP & FOX;	HARD WORK; SURVIVAL; MILITARY; WORKPLACE BULLYING
WHIP & BEAR;	FINANCIAL STRUGGLES; PERSONAL TRAINER; BODYBUILDING
WHIP & STARS:	TRAINING TO BE THE BEST; COACHING
WHIP & STORKS:	TOUGH NEW START; DIFFICULT AT THE BEGINNING; INITIAL EFFORT

WHIP & DOG:	FRIENDS WITH BENEFITS; TEASING; PERSONAL TRAINER
WHIP & TOWER:	GYM; LEGAL OR OFFICIAL DIFFICULTIES; FORTRESS
WHIP & GARDEN:	GROUP BULLYING; PEER PRESSURE; PUBLIC ARGUMENT
WHIP & MOUNTAIN:	MOUNTAIN-CLIMBING; SAFEGUARDING; LIMITATION; REALLY HARD WORK
WHIP & CROSSROAD:	DIFFICULT CHOICES; UNSETTLED; MULTIPLE ABUSES
WHIP & MICE:	ANXIETY; EXHAUSTION; STRESS
WHIP & HEART:	SEX; HEARTBREAK; LOVE CONFLICT
WHIP & RING:	DIFFICULT OR ABUSIVE RELATIONSHIP; HARSH CONTRACT
WHIP & BOOK:	HIDDEN SEXUALITY; HIDDEN ABUSE; ACADEMIC HARD WORK
WHIP & LETTER:	EROTIC FICTION; ABUSIVE MESSAGE, THREAT
WHIP & MAN:	MALE SEXUALITY; MALE ABUSER; FIT MAN; CRITIC
WHIP & WOMAN:	FEMALE SEXUALITY; FEMALE ABUSER; FIT WOMAN; CRITIC
WHIP & LILY:	AGEING TROUBLES; OLD AGE HARDSHIP; MATURE SEXUALITY
WHIP & SUN:	HARD WORK BRINGS SUCCESS; CHARISMA; VICTORY
WHIP & MOON:	EMOTIONAL ABUSE; DEPRESSION; OBSESSION; SEDUCTION
WHIP & KEY:	IMPORTANT LIFE LESSON; NECESSARY ACTION
WHIP & FISH:	BUSINESS DIFFICULTIES; MONEY FIGHTS; HARD WORK
WHIP & ANCHOR:	LONG-TERM HARDSHIP; CONSISTENT EFFORT
WHIP & CROSS:	SEVERE DEPRESSION; GUILT; SELF-FLAGELLATION

12. BIRDS

BIRDS & RIDER:	DELIVERY OF MESSAGES; RESPONSE; DISCUSSIONS
BIRDS & CLOVER:	CHANCE CONVERSATION; LUCKY COMMUNICATION
BIRDS & SHIP:	OVERSEAS NEGOTIATION; TALKING ABOUT A TRIP
BIRDS & HOUSE:	DOMESTIC DISCUSSIONS; HOUSE NEGOTIATIONS; FLATMATES
BIRDS & TREE	HEALTH DISCUSSION; KARMIC CONVERSATION
BIRDS & CLOUDS:	MIXED MESSAGES; MISCOMMUNICATION
BIRDS & SNAKE:	DECEITFUL CONVERSATION; BEING BUTTERED UP; GOSSIP
BIRDS & COFFIN:	FINAL COMMUNICATION; COMMUNICATION ENDS; SILENCE
BIRDS & BOUQUET:	LOVEBIRDS; PLEASANT CONVERSATION
BIRDS & SCYTHE:	CUTTING OFF COMMUNICATION; SPLIT
BIRDS & WHIP:	SEX-TALK; CHALLENGING CONVERSATION; ARGUMENTS
BIRDS & CHILD:	TALKING ABOUT PREGNANCY; BEGINNER'S TALK; KIDS' CHAT
BIRDS & FOX:	WORK CONVERSATION; DECEPTIVE CONVERSATION
BIRDS & BEAR:	FINANCIAL TALKS; MANAGER'S MEETING; MONEY TALK
BIRDS & STARS:	STAR INTERVIEW; PROMISING CHAT
BIRDS & STORKS:	INTRODUCTORY TALK; FRESH COMMUNICATION

BIRDS & DOG:	CONVERSATION WITH A FRIEND; FRIENDLY ADVICE
BIRDS & TOWER:	MEDIA ORGANIZATION; OFFICIAL COMMS; LEGAL DISCUSSION
BIRDS & GARDEN:	PUBLIC DISCUSSION; SOCIAL MEDIA; PUBLIC SPEAKING
BIRDS & MOUNTAIN:	COMMUNICATION DELAYS; BLOCKED COMMUNICATION
BIRDS & CROSSROAD:	MULTIPLE DISCUSSIONS; CHOICE OF COMMUNICATION; SPLIT
BIRDS & MICE:	ANXIOUS COUPLE; WORRIED COMMUNICATION
BIRDS & HEART:	LOVE BIRDS; ROMANTIC TALK; PASSIONATE CONVERSATION
BIRDS & RING:	PROPOSAL; DEALINGS; NEGOTIATIONS; AGREEMENT
BIRDS & BOOK:	SECRET CONVERSATION; SEMINAR; TEACHING
BIRDS & LETTER:	WRITTEN COMMUNICATION; MESSAGE; EMAIL
BIRDS & MAN:	MAN'S CONVERSATION; MALE COMMUNICATOR
BIRDS & WOMAN:	FEMALE CONVERSATION; FEMALE COMMUNICATOR
BIRDS & LILY:	MATURE DISCUSSION; GROWN-UPS TALKING; WISE WORDS
BIRDS & SUN:	MOTIVATIONAL SPEAKING; SUCCESSFUL CONVERSATION
BIRDS & MOON:	EMOTIONAL CONVERSATION; CREATIVE MEETING
BIRDS & KEY:	SIGNIFICANT CONVERSATION; KEY COMMUNICATION
BIRDS & FISH:	BUSINESS MEETING; BUSINESS CONVERSATION; SALES PITCH
BIRDS & ANCHOR:	LONG-TERM DISCUSSION; MEETING; TOGETHERNESS
BIRDS & CROSS:	COUNSELLING; RELIGIOUS TALK; WEIGHTY CONVERSATION

13. CHILD

CHILD & RIDER:	BIRTH ANNOUNCEMENT; NEW ARRIVAL
CHILD & CLOVER:	LUCKY CHILD; BEGINNER'S LUCK; SMALL PIECE OF LUCK
CHILD & SHIP:	TRIP WITH A CHILD; FOREIGN CHILD; SHORT TRIP
CHILD & HOUSE:	FAMILY HOME; DOLL'S HOUSE; BABYSITTING
CHILD & TREE:	GROWING CHILD; CHILDREN'S HEALTH; FERTILITY
CHILD & CLOUDS:	CONFUSED CHILD; UNCLEAR BEGINNER
CHILD & SNAKE:	UNTRUSTWORTHY KID; DIFFICULT CHILD; PROBLEM CHILD
CHILD & COFFIN:	CHILDHOOD ENDS; ABANDONED CHILD; MISCARRIAGE
CHILD & BOUQUET:	HAPPY CHILD; PLEASANT KID; ATTRACTIVE CHILD
CHILD & SCYTHE:	CHILDHOOD ACCIDENT; DECISIVE KID; SURGERY
CHILD & WHIP:	HARDWORKING CHILD; KID'S TRAINING; BULLY
CHILD & BIRDS:	CHATTY KID; SIBLINGS; PLAYMATES
CHILD & FOX:	SNEAKY KID; WORKING WITH CHILDREN; STARTER EMPLOYEE
CHILD & BEAR:	OVERWEIGHT CHILD; FINANCIAL BEGINNER; STRONG CHILD
CHILD & STARS	GIFTED CHILD; EARLY HIGH ACHIEVER
CHILD & STORKS:	BIRTH; NEW START FOR A CHILD; TOTAL BEGINNER

CHILD & DOG:	FRIENDLY KID; CHILDHOOD FRIEND
CHILD & TOWER:	SCHOOL; GOVERNING BODY; SOCIAL/CHILD SERVICES
CHILD & GARDEN:	PLAYMATES; CLASS; SOCIABLE CHILD; PEER-GROUP; DAY-CARE
CHILD & MOUNTAIN:	INFERTILITY; STRUGGLING CHILD; LONELY CHILD
CHILD & CROSSROAD:	SEVERAL CHILDREN; TWINS; NEW PATH
CHILD & MICE:	ANXIOUS OR NERVOUS CHILD
CHILD & HEART:	LOVING KID; LOVECHILD; YOUNGER RIVAL
CHILD & RING:	RELATIONSHIP WITH CHILD; ADOPTION
CHILD & BOOK	STUDENT, PUPIL; CLEVER CHILD; SCHOOL; SECRET CHILD
CHILD & LETTER:	NEWS OF A BIRTH; MESSAGE FROM A CHILD
CHILD & MAN:	CHILDISH MAN; MALE CHILD; MALE BEGINNER
CHILD & WOMAN:	CHILDISH WOMAN; FEMALE CHILD; FEMALE BEGINNER
CHILD & LILY:	OLD BEFORE THEIR TIME; ELDEST CHILD; MATURE BEGINNER
CHILD & SUN:	SUCCESSFUL CHILD; HIGH ACHIEVER; HAPPY CHILD
CHILD & MOON:	EMOTIONAL CHILD; CREATIVE KID
CHILD & KEY:	IMPORTANT CHILD; SUCCESSFUL CHILD; HEIR
CHILD & FISH:	BUSINESS BEGINNER; STARTUP; CHILD-RELATED BUSINESS
CHILD & ANCHOR:	SETTLED CHILD; RESPONSIBLE CHILD
CHILD & CROSS:	DEPRESSED CHILD; CHILDHOOD BURDEN

14. FOX

FOX & RIDER:	JOB OFFER; DOOR TO DOOR SALESMAN; NEW EMPLOYEE
FOX & CLOVER:	CHANCER; OPPORTUNIST; PROMOTION; JOB OPPORTUNITY;
FOX & SHIP:	TRAVEL FOR WORK; OVERSEAS EMPLOYEE; TRAVEL EMPLOYEE
FOX & HOUSE:	HOMEWORKER; DOMESTIC WORKER; FAMILY DECEIVER
FOX & TREE:	HEALTH-WORKER; DOCTOR; SPIRITUAL CHARLATAN
FOX & CLOUDS	JOB UNCERTAINTY; SOMEONE UNTRUSTWORTHY;
FOX & SNAKE:	CON ARTIST; BETRAYAL; DANGER
FOX & COFFIN:	JOB ENDS; LOSS OF EMPLOYMENT; MORTICIAN; UNDERTAKER
FOX & BOUQUET:	BEAUTY WORKER; PLEASANT JOB; NICE WORK; LOOKS CAN BE DECEPTIVE
FOX & SCYTHE:	REDUNDANCY; JOB LOSS; ACCIDENT AT WORK
FOX & WHIP:	HARSH JOB; TRAINING, COACHING
FOX & BIRDS:	INTERVIEW; COMMUNICATIONS JOB; LYING
FOX & CHILD:	JOB WITH CHILDREN; NEW EMPLOYEE; CUNNING CHILD
FOX & BEAR:	FINANCIAL JOB, ACCOUNTANCY; MANAGER; THEFT
FOX & STARS:	STAR EMPLOYEE; ASTRONAUT; AGENT, PUBLIC RELATIONS
FOX & STORKS	NEW JOB; JOB CHANGE; NEW START AT WORK

Fox & Dog:	COLLEAGUES; DISHONEST FRIEND
Fox & Tower	GOVERNMENT WORKER; PROFESSIONAL JOB; LAWYER;
Fox & Garden:	PUBLIC SECTOR WORKER; GARDENER; EVENTS WORK
Fox & Mountain:	UNEMPLOYMENT; BLOCKED WORK; MOUNTAINEER
Fox & Crossroad:	CAREER CHOICES; JOB OPTIONS; SMART DECISION
Fox & Mice:	WORK STRESS; JOB ANXIETY; JOB FEARS
Fox & Heart:	PASSIONATE WORK; ROMANTIC 'PLAYER'
Fox & Ring:	CONTRACT WORK; JOB CONTRACT; DODGY CONTRACT
Fox & Book:	PUBLISHER; LIBRARIAN; INVESTIGATOR; ACADEMIC
Fox & Letter:	POSTAL WORKER; WRITER; JOURNALIST; JOB NEWS; DECEPTIVE STORY
Fox & Man:	MALE EMPLOYEE; CON-MAN; MAN'S SURVIVAL
Fox & Woman:	FEMALE EMPLOYEE; CON-WOMAN; WOMAN'S SURVIVAL
Fox & Lily:	MATURE EMPLOYEE; EXPERIENCED WORKER
Fox & Sun:	SUCCESSFUL JOB-HUNT; SUCCESSFUL EMPLOYEE
Fox & Moon:	CREATIVE WORK, ARTS WORKER; EMOTIONAL JOB; PSYCHIC
Fox & Key:	IMPORTANT JOB; KEY EMPLOYEE
Fox & Fish:	FREELANCING/FREELANCER; BUSINESS ADVISOR
Fox & Anchor:	STABLE JOB; LONG-TERM EMPLOYMENT
Fox & Cross:	DEPRESSING WORK; PRESSURED JOB; CHARITY WORK

15. BEAR

Bear & Rider:	MONEY COMING: ARRIVAL OF POWERFUL VISITOR
Bear & Clover:	FINANCIAL GOOD FORTUNE; UNEXPECTED WINDFALL
Bear & Ship:	OVERSEAS MONEY; MONEY TRANSFER; HOLIDAY MONEY
Bear & House:	DOMESTIC FINANCES: SALE MONEY: FAMILY INHERITANCE
Bear & Tree:	NUTRITION; BODY BUILDING; FINANCIAL HEALTH
Bear & Clouds:	FINANCIAL UNCERTAINTY; CONFUSED FINANCES
Bear & Snake:	FRAUD; FINANCIAL DECEPTION
Bear & Coffin:	MONEY DRIES UP; POWER ENDING
Bear & Bouquet:	POSITIVE FINANCIAL SITUATION; PROSPERITY; NICE BOSS
Bear & Scythe:	SUDDEN FINANCIAL LOSSES; FINANCIAL DECISION
Bear & Whip:	GYM, TRAINING; FINANCIAL DIFFICULTIES; MONEY ROWS
Bear & Birds:	FINANCIAL DISCUSSION; TALKING ABOUT MONEY
Bear & Child:	CHILDHOOD OBESITY; FORCEFUL CHILD; TRUST FUND
Bear & Fox:	THEFT; FINANCIAL DECEPTION; SALARY
Bear & Stars:	FINANCIAL WIN; BONUS; CELEBRITY EARNINGS
Bear & Storks:	FINANCIAL NEW BEGINNING; NEW DIET

BEAR & DOG:	FINANCIAL HELP; LOAN; FRIENDLY BOSS; PERSONAL TRAINER
BEAR & TOWER:	GOVERNMENT FINANCE; LEGAL FEES; TAXES; BANK
BEAR & GARDEN:	PUBLIC FINANCES; PUBLIC POWER; KITTY, PUBLIC 'POT'
BEAR & MOUNTAIN:	BLOCKED INCOME; MONEY DELAYS; PREVENTED POWER
BEAR & CROSSROAD:	MULTIPLE SOURCES OF INCOME; FINANCIAL CHOICES
BEAR & MICE:	MONEY WORRIES; FINANCIAL LOSSES; WORRYING POWER
BEAR & HEART:	PHILANTHROPY; FINANCIAL GENEROSITY
BEAR & RING:	FINANCIAL DEAL; MARITAL FINANCES; STRONG BOND
BEAR & BOOK:	SECRET STASH; ACADEMIC FUNDING; FINANCIAL SECRECY
BEAR & LETTER:	CASH; FINANCIAL DOCUMENTS; BANK STATEMENT;
BEAR & MAN:	BIG MAN; MALE PROTECTION; MAN'S FINANCES; BOSS
BEAR & WOMAN;	POWERFUL WOMAN; MAMA BEAR; WOMAN'S FINANCES; BOSS
BEAR & LILY:	EXPERIENCED BOSS; INHERITANCE; PENSION;
BEAR & SUN:	GOOD FINANCIAL SITUATION; FINANCIAL SUCCESS
BEAR & MOON:	EMOTIONAL OR CREATIVE POWER; CREATIVE FUNDING
BEAR & KEY:	FINANCES ARE KEY; IMPORTANT MONEY; FINANCIAL SUCCESS
BEAR & FISH:	BUSINESS FINANCES; ACCOUNTS
BEAR & ANCHOR:	SAVINGS; NEST-EGG; LONG-TERM POWER
BEAR & CROSS	FINANCIAL BURDEN; MONEY WORRIES; TRAPPINGS OF POWER

16. STARS

STARS & RIDER:	DREAMS FULFILLED; ARRIVAL OF FAME; ACHIEVEMENT
STARS & CLOVER:	AMAZING LUCK; LUCKY STARS; PRIZE WIN
STAR & SHIP:	INTERNATIONAL FAME; DREAM TRIP; FOREIGN CELEB
STARS & HOUSE:	DREAM HOME; WELL-KNOWN FAMILY; FAMOUS HOUSE
STARS & TREE:	DESTINY; PROMISING RECOVERY
STARS & CLOUDS:	FANTASIES; ILLUSIONS; DREAMS
STARS & SNAKE:	FEMALE SEX-SYMBOL; DREAMS BETRAYED
STARS & COFFIN:	END OF HOPES AND DREAMS; HOPES DASHED
STARS & BOUQUET:	AWARD; POSITIVE ACHIEVEMENT; ACCOLADES; FAME
STARS & SCYTHE:	SWIFT ACTION TOWARDS GOALS; DECISIVE ACHIEVEMENT
STARS & WHIP:	HARD-WORKING HIGH ACHIEVER; DIVA; SPORTSPERSON
STARS & BIRDS:	PUBLIC RELATIONS; NETWORKING; TOP-LEVEL TALKS
STARS & CHILD:	CHILD STAR; SPOILT CHILD; SUCCESSFUL BEGINNER
STARS & FOX:	STAR EMPLOYEE; BLAGGER; CELEBRITY PROMOTION
STARS & BEAR:	FINANCIAL GURU; MONEY GOALS; POWERFUL CELEB
STARS & STORKS:	HOPES OF A NEW BEGINNING; RISING STAR

STARS & DOG:	BEST FRIENDS; FAMOUS FRIENDS
STARS & TOWER:	A-LIST CELEB; ESTABLISHED STAR; REACHING FOR THE STARS
STARS & GARDEN:	WELL-CONNECTED; NATIONAL TREASURE; GLITTERING PARTY
STARS & MOUNTAIN:	BLOCKED DREAMS; HARD TO REACH GOALS
STARS & CROSSROAD:	CHOICE OF GOALS; SUCCESSFUL CHOICE
STARS & MICE:	STAGE FRIGHT; WORRIES ABOUT REPUTATION
STARS & HEART:	CRUSH; OBJECT OF AFFECTIONS
STARS & RING:	TOP RELATIONSHIP; MARRIAGE HOPES; CONTRACT GOALS
STARS & BOOK:	CHARACTERS; BESTSELLER; HIDDEN GOALS; ACADEMIC ACHIEVEMENT
STARS & LETTER:	GOOD NEWS; REFERENCE; CERTIFICATE
STARS & MAN:	MALE CELEB; POPULAR MAN; SUCCESSFUL MAN
STARS & WOMAN:	FEMALE CELEB; SUCCESSFUL WOMAN; POPULAR WOMAN
STARS & LILY:	LATE BLOOMER; OLDER CELEB
STARS & SUN:	HUGE SUCCESS; BIG ACHIEVEMENT; HONOUR
STARS & MOON:	CREATIVE GOALS; FAME; IDEAS
STARS & KEY:	WINNER; "THE ONE"; SIGNIFICANT GOALS; DESTINED FAME
STARS & FISH:	SUCCESSFUL ENTREPRENEUR; FINANCIAL GOALS
STARS & ANCHOR:	ESTABLISHED STAR; LEGENDARY
STARS & CROSS:	FATE; TROUBLED CELEB

17. STORKS

STORK & RIDER:	NEW BEGINNING UPCOMING; THE ARRIVAL OF SOMEONE NEW
STORK & CLOVER:	OPPORTUNITY FOR A FRESH START; LUCKY NEW BEGINNING
STORK & SHIP:	FIRST LEG OF A TRIP; JOURNEY BEGINS; TRAVELLING AFRESH
STORK & HOUSE:	HOUSE MOVE; FRESH START FOR THE FAMILY
STORK & TREE:	NEW LEASE OF LIFE; RECOVERY; HEALTH IMPROVES
STORK & CLOUDS:	RISKY NEW START; TAKE THINGS AS THEY COME; UNFOCUSED
STORK & SNAKE:	PROBLEMATIC BEGINNING; TROUBLED START
STORK & COFFIN:	FALSE START; CANCELLATION;
STORK & BOUQUET:	HAPPY FRESH START; IMPROVEMENTS; POSITIVE CHANGES
STORK & SCYTHE:	UNEXPECTED OR SUDDEN CHANGE
STORK & WHIP:	TOUGH BEGINNING; DIFFICULT CHANGE
STORK & BIRDS:	NEWS OF CHANGE; TALKING ABOUT FRESH START;
STORK & CHILD:	BIRTH; PREGNANCY; BEGINNER
STORK & FOX:	CHANGE OF JOB; NEW START AT WORK
STORK & BEAR:	FINANCIAL FRESH START; POWERFUL CHANGE
STORK & STARS:	RISING STAR; HOPEFUL NEW BEGINNING; PROGRESS

STORK & DOG:	NEW FRIENDSHIP; RENEWED LOYALTY
STORK & TOWER:	CHANGES AT THE TOP; NEW GOVERNMENT
STORK & GARDEN:	GROUP CHANGES OR BEGINS; PUBLIC CHANGE
STORK & MOUNTAIN:	START DELAYED; OBSTACLES TO CHANGE
STORK & CROSSROAD:	NEW PATHS AHEAD; FRESH OPTIONS
STORK & MICE:	WORRYING CHANGES; FIRST DAY NERVES
STORK & HEART:	NEW ROMANCE; RELATIONSHIP FRESH START
STORK & RING:	HONEYMOON PERIOD; NEW CONTRACT; PROMISE
STORK & BOOK:	LEARNING SOMETHING NEW; FRESH LEAD
STORK & LETTER:	NEWS OF CHANGE; SIGN-OFF RECEIVED
STORK & MAN:	NEW START FOR A MAN; FLEXIBLE MAN; PROGRESSIVE
STORK & WOMAN:	NEW START FOR A WOMAN; FLEXIBLE WOMAN; PROGRESSIVE
STORK & LILY:	LATER LIFE CHANGES; MATURITY
STORK & SUN:	SUCCESSFUL NEW START; SUCCESSFUL CHANGES
STORK & MOON:	CREATIVE START; EMOTIONAL NEW BEGINNING; HAPPINESS
STORK & KEY:	SIGNIFICANT START; IMPORTANT CHANGE; LIFE-CHANGING
STORK & FISH:	EARLY-STAGE BUSINESS; BUSINESS CHANGE
STORK & ANCHOR:	STABLE BEGINNING; LONG TERM PROGRESS
STORK & CROSS:	DIFFICULT START; UNPLEASANT CHANGE; HARDER THAN ANTICIPATED

18. DOG

Dog & Rider:	VISIT FROM A FRIEND; SOMEONE NEW ARRIVES IN YOUR LIFE
Dog & Clover:	LUCKY FRIENDSHIP OR FRIEND; FRIEND BRINGS LUCK
Dog & Ship:	OVERSEAS FRIEND; TRAVELLING COMPANION
Dog & House:	FAITHFUL PARTNER; FAMILY FRIEND; COMPANION
Dog & Tree:	KARMIC RETURN; FIT FRIEND; GROWING SUPPORT
Dog & Clouds:	DODGY FRIEND; CONFUSED FRIEND
Dog & Snake:	BETRAYAL FROM SOMEONE YOU TRUST; DISLOYALTY
Dog & Coffin:	END OF A FRIENDSHIP; END-OF-LIFE SUPPORT
Dog & Bouquet:	HAPPY FRIENDSHIP; GOOD-LOOKING FRIEND
Dog & Scythe:	ABANDONMENT; CUT-OFF FRIENDSHIP; DECISIVE FRIEND
Dog & Whip:	FRIENDS-WITH-BENEFITS; HARSH FRIEND; TRAINER, COACH
Dog & Birds:	CHATTY FRIEND; TALKING WITH FRIENDS; FLATMATES
Dog & Child:	CHILDHOOD FRIEND; YOUNG FRIENDSHIP
Dog & Fox:	COLLEAGUE; SNEAKY FRIEND
Dog & Bear:	WEALTHY FRIEND; FINANCIAL ADVISOR; BODYGUARD
Dog & Stars:	FAMOUS FRIEND; HIGH-FLIER YOU KNOW; BEST PAL

DOG & STORKS	FRESH START IN A FRIENDSHIP; START OF A NEW FRIENDSHIP
DOG & TOWER:	FRIENDS IN HIGH PLACES; OFFICIAL ADVISER; LAWYER
DOG & GARDEN:	GROUP OF FRIENDS; PARTY, CELEBRATION
DOG & MOUNTAIN:	BLOCKED FRIENDSHIP; HARD-GOING FRIENDSHIP
DOG & CROSSROAD:	LOTS OF FRIENDS; CHOICE OF FRIENDS; GUIDE OR MENTOR
DOG & MICE:	ANXIOUS FRIEND; STRESSFUL FRIENDSHIP
DOG & HEART:	GREAT FRIEND; SOULMATE; CLOSE BUDDY; LIFE PARTNER
DOG & RING:	PARTNER; MARRIED FRIEND; LIFE COMPANION; ALLY
DOG & BOOK:	SECRET FRIEND; CLASSMATE; FELLOW RESEARCHER
DOG & LETTER:	PENPAL; INTERNET FRIEND
DOG & MAN:	MALE FRIEND; MALE FRIENDSHIPS; MAN AND PARTNER
DOG & WOMAN:	FEMALE FRIEND; FEMALE FRIENDSHIPS; WOMAN AND
DOG & LILY:	OLD FRIEND; LIFELONG COMPANION
DOG & SUN:	POSITIVE FRIENDSHIP; SUCCESSFUL FRIEND
DOG & MOON:	EMOTIONAL FRIENDSHIP; CREATIVE COLLEAGUE
DOG & KEY:	SIGNIFICANT FRIEND; PAST LIFE RETURN
DOG & FISH:	BUSINESS ASSOCIATE; MENTOR; ADVISER
DOG & ANCHOR:	STABLE FRIENDSHIP; RELIABLE FRIEND
DOG & CROSS:	DIFFICULT OR CO-DEPENDENT FRIENDSHIP; COUNSELLING

19. TOWER

TOWER & RIDER:	ARRIVAL OF AUTHORITIES; OFFICIAL VISIT; AUTHORITARIAN
TOWER & CLOVER:	LUCKY ORGANIZATION; SUCCESSFUL COMPANY; CASINO
TOWER & SHIP:	GLOBAL CORPORATION; VISA REQUIREMENTS; AIRPORT
TOWER & HOUSE:	CASTLE; FLATS; ESTATE AGENTS; GOVT DEPARTMENT
TOWER & TREE:	HEALTH CENTRE, HOSPITAL; DEPARTMENT OF HEALTH, N.H.S.
TOWER & CLOUDS:	SHADY AUTHORITIES; PROPAGANDISTS; MAFIA
TOWER & SNAKE:	UNTRUSTWORTHY ORGANIZATION; CORRUPTION;
TOWER & COFFIN:	MAUSOLEUM, FUNERAL PARLOUR; FALL OF GOVERNMENT
TOWER & BOUQUET:	BEAUTY OR FASHION INDUSTRY; BEAUTIFUL BUILDING
TOWER & SCYTHE:	GOVERNMENT CUTS; LOSS OF STATURE; OFFICIAL DECISION
TOWER & WHIP:	TOUGH OFFICIALS; PRISON; GYM; STRUGGLE FOR STATUS
TOWER & BIRDS:	PARLIAMENT; OFFICIAL NEWS; LEGAL TALKS
TOWER & CHILD:	CHILDREN'S ORGANIZATION; SCHOOL
TOWER & FOX	CORPORATE WORK; OFFICIAL BUSINESS; LAWYER; DECEITFUL OFFICIAL
TOWER & BEAR:	BANK; TAX OFFICE; TREASURY; POWERFUL ORGANISATION
TOWER & STARS:	STAR STATUS; BIG EGO; PR MACHINE

TOWER & STORKS:	GETTING ESTABLISHED; MAKING IT OFFICIAL; NEW GOVT
TOWER & DOG:	ANIMAL SHELTER; OFFICIAL SUPPORT, FRIENDLY OFFICIAL
TOWER & GARDEN:	PUBLIC ORGANIZATION; PUBLIC BUILDING
TOWER & MOUNTAIN:	BLOCKED BY OFFICIALS; INSURMOUNTABLE DELAYS
TOWER & CROSSROAD	ORGANISATIONAL CHOICES; OFFICIAL DIRECTION
TOWER & MICE:	CRUMBLING STRUCTURE; CORPORATE WORRIES
TOWER & HEART:	DATING ORGANIZATION; CHARITABLE ORGANISATION
TOWER & RING:	GOVERNMENT CONTRACT; CORPORATE DEAL
TOWER & BOOK:	SCHOOL, COLLEGE, UNIVERSITY; BIG PUBLISHER
TOWER & LETTER:	POST OFFICE; NEWS ORGANIZATION; OFFICIAL NOTICE
TOWER & MAN:	MALE OFFICIAL; GURU FIGURE; EXPERT
TOWER & WOMAN:	FEMALE OFFICIAL; WOMAN'S STATUS; EXPERT
TOWER & LILY	OLD PEOPLE'S CHARITY; ESTABLISHED ORGANISATION
TOWER & SUN:	'MAKING IT'; SUCCESSFUL ORGANIZATION; HIGH STATUS
TOWER & MOON:	EMOTIONAL WITHDRAWAL; CREATIVE ORGANISATION
TOWER & KEY:	GOVERNMENT; SIGNIFICANT ORGANIZATION; MAJOR CORPORATION
TOWER & FISH:	BUSINESS REGISTRY; TRADE ORGANISATION
TOWER & ANCHOR:	LONG TERM STATUS; ESTABLISHMENT
TOWER & CROSS:	CHURCH; DIFFICULTY WITH AUTHORITIES

20. GARDEN

GARDEN & RIDER:	PARTY INVITE; A MORE SOCIABLE PERIOD; VISITORS
GARDEN & CLOVER:	FORTUNATE GROUP; LUCKY EVENT
GARDEN & SHIP:	TRAVEL COMPANIONS; GROUP HOLIDAY
GARDEN & HOUSE:	HOUSE PARTY; DOMESTIC GATHERING; LARGE FAMILY
GARDEN & TREE:	KARMIC MEETING; PUBLIC HEALTH; SPA
GARDEN & CLOUDS:	DIFFICULT CROWD; PROBLEMS IN A GROUP
GARDEN & SNAKE:	SNAKE IN THE GRASS; BETRAYAL IN A GROUP
GARDEN & COFFIN:	END OF SOCIABILITY; PARTY CANCELLATION; SOCIAL SHAME
GARDEN & BOUQUET:	LOVELY GATHERING; PLEASANT MEETING; GARDEN PARTY
GARDEN & SCYTHE:	PUBLIC DECISION OR WILL; OSTRACISM; RECLUSIVENESS
GARDEN & WHIP:	UNFORGIVING PUBLIC; ARGUMENT; ORGY; TRAINING GROUP
GARDEN & BIRDS:	PUBLIC SPEECH; DISCUSSION GROUP; SOCIAL MEDIA
GARDEN & CHILD:	CLASS; SCHOOL-FRIENDS; PLAYGROUP; BEGINNER'S GROUP
GARDEN & FOX:	WORK COLLEAGUES AND ASSOCIATES; NETWORK
GARDEN & BEAR:	MARKETPLACE; PRIZE DRAW
GARDEN & STARS:	GALA; AWARD CEREMONY; CONSTELLATION; FANS

GARDEN & STORKS:	A NEW CROWD OR NETWORK; PUBLIC FRESH START
GARDEN & DOG:	FRIENDSHIP GROUP; SUPPORTIVE NETWORK
GARDEN & TOWER:	ORGANISATIONS; PUBLIC BUILDING; LEADERSHIP
GARDEN & MOUNTAIN:	BLOCKED SOCIABILITY; CANCELLATION OF EVENT
GARDEN & CROSSROAD:	PUBLIC OPTIONS; CHOICE OF SOCIAL GROUPS
GARDEN & MICE:	ANXIOUS PUBLIC; WORRIED ASSOCIATES
GARDEN & HEART:	DATING POOL; PUBLIC ROMANTIC EVENT
GARDEN & RING:	MEMBERSHIP; WEDDING
GARDEN & BOOK:	COLLEGE; HIDDEN NETWORK; KNOWLEDGE SHARING
GARDEN & LETTER:	ANNOUNCEMENT; PUBLIC DOCUMENTS; INVITATION
GARDEN & MAN:	SOCIABLE MAN; MALE GROUP; MEN AS A WHOLE
GARDEN & WOMAN:	SOCIABLE WOMAN; FEMALE GROUP; WOMEN AS A WHOLE
GARDEN & LILY:	LONGSTANDING NETWORK; OLDER GROUP; MATURE GATHERING
GARDEN & SUN:	SUCCESSFUL SUPPORT NETWORK; PUBLIC SUCCESS
GARDEN & MOON:	AUDIENCE FOR CREATIVITY; PUBLIC; SUPPORT GROUP
GARDEN & KEY:	SIGNIFICANT NETWORK; PUBLIC IMPORTANCE
GARDEN & FISH:	BUSINESS ASSOCIATES; NETWORKING
GARDEN & ANCHOR:	STABLE ASSOCIATIONS; LONG-TERM GROUP
GARDEN & CROSS:	THERAPY GROUP; RELIGIOUS CONGREGATION

21. MOUNTAIN

MOUNTAIN & RIDER:	DELAYED ARRIVAL; LATE DELIVERY
MOUNTAIN & CLOVER:	EVENTUAL LUCK; THINGS IMPROVE
MOUNTAIN & SHIP:	JOURNEY DELAY; CANCELLED TRIP
MOUNTAIN & HOUSE:	ISOLATION; PROBLEMS WITH HOUSE SALE
MOUNTAIN & TREE:	HEALTH ISSUES; DELAYS IN RECOVERY
MOUNTAIN & CLOUDS:	CONFUSIONS AND BLOCKAGES; HIDDEN OBSTACLE
MOUNTAIN & SNAKE:	PROBLEMS AND DELAYS
MOUNTAIN & COFFIN:	FINALITY; END OF OBSTACLES
MOUNTAIN & BOUQUET:	MOUNTAIN RESORT; TAKING THE SCENIC ROUTE
MOUNTAIN & SCYTHE:	ACTION AFTER BLOCKAGE
MOUNTAIN & WHIP:	TOUGH TIMES; STRUGGLE
MOUNTAIN & BIRDS:	BLOCKED CONVERSATION; DELAYED MEETING
MOUNTAIN & CHILD:	SMALL OBSTACLE; ISOLATED CHILD; LATE STARTER
MOUNTAIN & FOX:	WORK DELAYS; BLOCKED CAREER
MOUNTAIN & BEAR:	FINANCIAL DELAYS; INCOME BLOCKED
MOUNTAIN & STARS:	CHALLENGING GOALS; ACHIEVEMENTS BLOCKED

MOUNTAIN & STORKS;	FRESH START DELAYED; FALSE START; ON THE MOVE AGAIN
MOUNTAIN & DOG:	BLOCKED FRIENDSHIP; ABANDONMENT
MOUNTAIN & TOWER:	OFFICIAL DELAYS; LEGAL RESTRICTION; PRISON
MOUNTAIN & GARDEN	GROUP BLOCKED, SLOWED DOWN
MOUNTAIN & CROSSROAD:	CHOICES BLOCKED; MULTIPLE DELAYS
MOUNTAIN & MICE:	ANXIETIES AND DELAYS; BETA BLOCKERS
MOUNTAIN & HEART:	LOVE BLOCKAGE; LONELY HEART
MOUNTAIN & RING:	RELATIONSHIP PREVENTED; CONTRACT DELAYS
MOUNTAIN & BOOK:	HIDDEN BLOCKAGE; KNOWLEDGE BLOCKED
MOUNTAIN & LETTER:	DELAYED MESSAGE
MOUNTAIN & MAN:	ISOLATED MAN; MAN CAUSES DELAYS
MOUNTAIN & WOMAN:	ISOLATED WOMAN; WOMAN CAUSES DELAYS
MOUNTAIN & LILY:	SLOWING DOWN IN OLD AGE; TAKING THINGS EASY
MOUNTAIN & SUN:	SUCCESS AFTER DELAY; SOMETHING SUCCESSFULLY PREVENTED
MOUNTAIN & MOON:	CREATIVE BLOCKAGE; PENT-UP EMOTIONS
MOUNTAIN & KEY:	SIGNIFICANT DELAY; BLOCKS OVERCOME
MOUNTAIN & FISH:	BUSINESS DELAY; FREEDOM PREVENTED; BUSINESS BLOCK
MOUNTAIN & ANCHOR:	STAGNANT; LONG-TERM BLOCKAGE; PERMANENT STOP
MOUNTAIN & CROSS:	DEPRESSION; INSURMOUNTABLE TROUBLE

22. CROSSROADS

Crossroad & Rider: Arrival of options; choice to be made; messages

Crossroad & Clover: Fortunate path; lucky choices; positive ways ahead

Crossroad & Ship: Journey options; choice of direction; route or map

Crossroad & House: Choice of home; family options; domestic choices

Crossroad & Tree: Health options or outcomes; karmic path; spiritual directions

Crossroad & Clouds: The way forward is unclear; uncertainty; can't see way ahead

Crossroad & Snake: A wrong turning; difficult choices; no positive options

Crossroad & Coffin: The end of the road; no choice; final options

Crossroad & Bouquet: Pleasant choices; happy outcome; positive roads ahead

Crossroad & Scythe: Decisiveness; road accident; reduced options

Crossroad & Whip: Tough choices; forced options; limited roads ahead

Crossroad & Birds: Phone line; network; communication options

Crossroad & Child: Child's choices; early options; siblings; child's future

Crossroad & Fox: Career crossroads; job options; multiple jobs; clever choices

Crossroad & Bear: Financial options; several income streams

Crossroad & Stars: Path to achievement; goal-making; ambitious road ahead

CROSSROAD & STORKS:	NEW DIRECTION; PROGRESS; NEW ROADS OPENING UP
CROSSROAD & DOG:	CHOICE OF COMPANION; FRIENDSHIP PATH; HELPFUL GUIDANCE
CROSSROAD & TOWER:	OFFICIAL PATHWAYS; LEGAL OPTIONS; GOVERNMENT CHOICES
CROSSROAD & GARDEN:	SOCIABILITY; PARTIES; CHOICE OF EVENTS
CROSSROAD & MOUNTAIN	ANALYSIS PARALYSIS; ALL AVENUES BLOCKED
CROSSROAD & MICE:	OVERWHELM, TOO MANY OPTIONS; STRESS
CROSSROAD & HEART:	SEVERAL LOVE INTERESTS; DATING OPTIONS; ROMANTIC CHOICES
CROSSROAD & RING:	RELATIONSHIP CHOICE; CONTRACT OFFERS
CROSSROAD & BOOK:	SECRET PATHWAY; LEARNING OPTIONS; DISCOVERY; WHAT TO READ NEXT
CROSSROAD & LETTER:	MESSAGES SENT OUT; MAILING OPTIONS; NEWSLETTERS
CROSSROAD & MAN:	MAN'S DECISIONS; NON-COMMITTAL
CROSSROAD & WOMAN:	WOMAN'S DECISIONS; NON-COMMITTAL
CROSSROAD & LILY:	MATURE CHOICES; PEACEFUL PATH
CROSSROAD & SUN:	SUCCESSFUL ROUTE; RIGHT CHOICE
CROSSROAD & MOON:	CREATIVE OPTIONS; EMOTIONAL CROSSROADS
CROSSROAD & KEY:	SIGNIFICANT CHOICES; KEY TURNING POINT
CROSSROAD & FISH:	MULTIPLE BUSINESSES; BUSINESS OPTIONS
CROSSROAD & ANCHOR:	STABLE CHOICES; LONG TERM ROAD AHEAD
CROSSROAD & CROSS:	TOUGH ROAD AHEAD; NO EASY CHOICE

23. MICE

MICE & RIDER:	TROUBLES AFOOT; VISITOR ANXIETY; WORRYING
MICE & CLOVER:	BUTTERFLIES; ANXIOUS ANTICIPATION; TRUST YOUR GUT
MICE & SHIP:	FEAR OF FLYING; ANXIOUS TRIP; PROBLEMS ON A JOURNEY
MICE & HOUSE:	DOMESTIC NIGGLES; HOUSE WORRIES; FAMILY ISSUES
MICE & TREE:	HEALTH CONCERNS; SYMPTOMS OF ANXIETY
MICE & CLOUDS:	LACK OF CLARITY CAUSES ANXIETY; DISTRESS; CONFUSION
MICE & SNAKE:	MAJOR PROBLEMS; PARANOIA
MICE & COFFIN:	WORRIES END; ANXIETY ABOUT AN ENDING; MORBIDITY
MICE & BOUQUET:	ANTICIPATION; NERVOUS EXCITEMENT; THRILL
MICE & SCYTHE:	ANXIETY ABOUT A DECISION; BREAKUP WORRIES
MICE & WHIP	STRESS AND PRESSURE; ARGUMENTS CAUSE ANXIETY
MICE & BIRDS	FEAR OF COMMUNICATION; WORRIED ABOUT A MEETING
MICE & CHILD:	WORRIED ABOUT A CHILD; SMALL PROBLEMS
MICE & FOX:	JOB WORRIES; CAREER ANXIETY; WORK STRESS
MICE & BEAR:	MONEY WORRIES; FINANCIAL STRESS
MICE & STARS:	PERFORMANCE ANXIETY; PRESSURE

MICE & STORKS:	ANXIOUS ABOUT CHANGE; UNWANTED NEW START
MICE & DOG:	FRIENDSHIP WORRIES; ANXIOUS FRIEND
MICE & TOWER:	OFFICIAL CONCERNS; LEGAL WORRIES
MICE & GARDEN:	SOCIAL ANXIETY; AGORAPHOBIA
MICE & MOUNTAIN:	DELAYED ANXIETY; LONG TERM STRESS; PTSD
MICE & CROSSROAD:	OPTION OVERLOAD; ANXIOUS OVER WHAT TO DO NEXT
MICE & HEART:	LOVE WORRIES; ROMANTIC PROBLEMS; RELATIONSHIP STRESS
MICE & RING:	CONTRACT DIFFICULTIES; MARRIAGE TROUBLES
MICE & BOOK:	SECRET WORRIES;; STUDY STRESS
MICE & LETTER:	TROUBLING NEWS; DOCUMENTED CONCERNS
MICE & MAN:	MAN'S WORRIES; STRESSED MAN
MICE & WOMAN:	WOMAN'S WORRIES; STRESSED WOMAN
MICE & LILY:	AGEING WORRIES; DEMENTIA
MICE & SUN:	ANXIOUS ABOUT SUCCESS; EVENTUAL VICTORY
MICE & MOON:	EMOTIONAL TROUBLES; CREATIVE CONCERNS
MICE & KEY:	SIGNIFICANT CONCERN; IMPORTANT WORRIES
MICE & FISH:	BUSINESS PROBLEMS; FREELANCER WORRIES
MICE & ANCHOR:	LONG-TERM ANXIETY; CONSTANT STATE OF WORRY
MICE & CROSS	TROUBLED; BURDENED; MAJOR ANXIETY

24. HEART

HEART & RIDER:	NEW LOVER; ARRIVAL OF ROMANCE
HEART & CLOVER:	LUCKY ROMANCE; HAPPY LOVE LIFE
HEART & SHIP:	ROMANTIC TRIP; HOLIDAY ROMANCE
HEART & HOUSE:	HEARTH & HOME; DOMESTIC BLISS; LOVING FAMILY
HEART & TREE:	HEALTHY HEART; KARMIC LOVE; GROWING ROMANCE
HEART & CLOUDS:	CONFUSING ROMANCE; UNCLEAR ROMANTIC INTENTIONS
HEART & SNAKE:	ROMANTIC BETRAYAL; CHEATING HEART
HEART & COFFIN:	END OF A ROMANCE; BROKEN HEART
HEART & BOUQUET:	BLOSSOMING LOVE; ROMANTIC HAPPINESS; WEDDING
HEART & SCYTHE:	HEARTBROKEN; DAMAGED HEART; HEART SURGERY
HEART & WHIP:	SEXUAL DESIRE; TOUGH LOVE; CHALLENGING ROMANCE;
HEART & BIRDS:	SWEET-TALK; ROMANTIC CONVERSATION; LOVEBIRDS
HEART & CHILD:	CHILD'S LOVE; CHILDLIKE LOVE; YOUNG LOVE
HEART & FOX:	STOLEN HEART; CAREER PASSIONS; PLAYER; DECEPTIVE LOVE
HEART & BEAR	PROTECTIVE LOVE; FINANCIAL PROVIDER; POWERFUL LOVE
HEART & STARS:	CELEBRITY CRUSH; IDEALISTIC LOVE

HEART & STORKS:	NEW ROMANCE BEGINNING; STARTING TO DATE AGAIN
HEART & DOG:	FAITHFUL LOVE; SOULMATE; FIDELITY
HEART & TOWER:	MAKING IT OFFICIAL; HIGH-STATUS ROMANCE; CORE VALUES
HEART & GARDEN:	WEDDING; GOING PUBLIC WITH ROMANCE; FANDOM
HEART & MOUNTAIN:	BLOCKED ROMANCE; HARD-HEARTED; LONELY HEART
HEART & CROSSROAD:	ROMANTIC OPTIONS; CHOICE OF PASSIONS
HEART & MICE:	ROMANTIC ANXIETIES; ANXIOUS, CLINGY ROMANCE
HEART & RING:	MARRIAGE; ENGAGEMENT; MARRIED LOVE
HEART & BOOK:	SECRET ROMANCE; AFFAIR; ACADEMIC PASSION
HEART & LETTER:	LOVE LETTER; ROMANTIC MESSAGE; LOVE POEM
HEART & MAN:	MALE LOVER; PARTNER; MAN'S LOVE
HEART & WOMAN:	FEMALE LOVER; PARTNER; WOMAN'S LOVE
HEART & LILY:	ENDURING LOVE; LATER-LIFE ROMANCE; WISE HEART
HEART & SUN:	HAPPY ROMANCE; JOYFUL LOVE
HEART & MOON:	ROMANTIC LOVE; EMOTIVE ROMANCE; CREATIVE PASSION
HEART & KEY:	SIGNIFICANT LOVE; THE ONE; DESTINED; SOULMATE
HEART & FISH:	FREE AGENT; NO-STRINGS AFFAIR; BUSINESS PASSION
HEART & ANCHOR:	LONG-LASTING LOVE; LONG-TERM ROMANCE
HEART & CROSS:	TROUBLED ROMANCE; CODEPENDENCY; HEAVY HEART

25. RING

RING & RIDER:	CONTRACT ON THE WAY; NEW DEAL; PROPOSAL
RING & CLOVER:	FORTUNATE CONTRACT; LUCKY DEAL; HAPPY MARRIAGE
RING & SHIP:	OVERSEAS CONTRACT; TRAVEL BOOKING
RING & HOUSE:	RENTAL AGREEMENT; HOUSE SALE; FAMILY RELATIONSHIPS
RING & TREE:	KARMIC RETURN; BUDDING RELATIONSHIP; SPIRITUAL LINK
RING & CLOUDS:	BAD CONTRACT; UNCLEAR TERMS; CONFUSING RELATIONSHIP
RING & SNAKE:	UNTRUSTWORTHY CONTRACT; BETRAYED MARRIAGE
RING & COFFIN:	END OF A CONTRACT; RELATIONSHIP OVER
RING & BOUQUET:	WEDDING; HAPPY RELATIONSHIP; AGREEABLE CONTRACT
RING & SCYTHE:	BREAK-UP; CUT TIES; BROKEN CONTRACT;
RING & WHIP:	TOUGH TERMS; ARGUMENTATIVE OR ABUSIVE RELATIONSHIP
RING & BIRDS:	NEGOTIATION; RELATIONSHIP DISCUSSION;
RING & CHILD:	ADOPTION; PARENTAL BOND; CHILD'S RELATIONSHIP
RING & FOX:	WORK AGREEMENT; WILY CONTRACT
RING & BEAR:	PAYMENT; FINANCIAL CONTRACT; POWERFUL RELATIONSHIP
RING & STARS:	CELEB MARRIAGE; HIGH PROFILE CONTRACT; STICK TO GOALS

RING & STORKS:	FRESH MARRIAGE OR RELATIONSHIP; NEW CONTRACT
RING & DOG:	FRIENDLY AGREEMENT; STRONG FRIENDSHIP;
RING & TOWER:	OFFICIAL AGREEMENT, SIGNED CONTRACT; LEGAL TERMS
RING & GARDEN:	GROUP MEMBERSHIP; PUBLIC AGREEMENT; WEDDING PARTY
RING & MOUNTAIN:	OBSTACLES TO AGREEMENT; DELAYED MARRIAGE
RING & CROSSROAD:	BIGAMY; AGREEMENT OPTIONS; CHOICE OF CONTRACTS
RING & MICE:	ANXIOUS RELATIONSHIP; UNHAPPILY MARRIED
RING & HEART:	ROMANTIC COMMITMENT, MARRIAGE; LOVE PARTNERSHIP
RING & BOOK:	SECRET AGREEMENT; HIDDEN TERMS; BOOK DEAL
RING & LETTER:	WRITTEN AGREEMENT; CERTIFICATE; WEDDING INVITE
RING & MAN:	HUSBAND; MAN'S MARRIAGE; MAN'S WORD
RING & WOMAN:	WIFE, WOMAN'S MARRIAGE; WOMAN'S WORD
RING & LILY:	MATURE AGREEMENT; OLDER MARRIAGE
RING & SUN:	SUCCESSFUL RELATIONSHIP; HAPPY MARRIAGE; GOOD DEAL
RING & MOON:	EMOTIONAL RELATIONSHIP; CREATIVE AGREEMENT
RING & KEY:	KEY RELATIONSHIP; DESTINY, KARMA; IMPORTANT CONTRACT
RING & FISH:	BUSINESS DEAL; PAYMENT
RING & ANCHOR:	STABLE RELATIONSHIP OR MARRIAGE; SECURITY; LONG TERM AGREEMENT
RING & CROSS	WEIGHED-DOWN RELATIONSHIP; OPPRESSIVE DEAL

26. BOOK

BOOK & RIDER:	KNOWLEDGE OR INFORMATION ARRIVES
BOOK & CLOVER:	LUCKY KNOWLEDGE; FORTUNATE SECRET; GREAT DISCOVERY
BOOK & SHIP:	EXPLORATION; FOREIGN LEARNING; TRAVEL GUIDE
BOOK & HOUSE:	FAMILY SECRET; D.I.Y. MANUAL; FAMILY KNOWLEDGE
BOOK & TREE:	SPIRITUAL KNOWLEDGE; HEALTH SECRET; HIDDEN ILLNESS
BOOK & CLOUDS:	MISINTERPRETATION; OBSCURED KNOWLEDGE; INCORRECT
BOOK & SNAKE:	FALSE INFORMATION; BETRAYED SECRET
BOOK & COFFIN:	LEARNING ENDS; SECRET UNCOVERED
BOOK & BOUQUET:	PLEASANT DISCOVERY; BEAUTY SECRETS; LEARNING
BOOK & SCYTHE:	SUDDEN REVEAL; HURTFUL SECRET; RAPID LEARNING
BOOK & WHIP:	SEX SECRET; HIDDEN ABUSE; TOUGH SCHOOLING
BOOK & BIRDS:	GOSSIP; STORYTELLING; LECTURE, CLASS; AUDIO-BOOK
BOOK & CHILD	SCHOOLWORK; BEGINNER'S MANUAL; CHILD'S SECRET
BOOK & FOX:	WORK SECRET; JOB KNOWLEDGE; ACADEMIC AUTHOR
BOOK & BEAR	FINANCIAL KNOWLEDGE; POWERFUL SECRET; ACCOUNTS
BOOK & STARS	CELEB SECRET, TOP EDUCATION; BESTSELLER

BOOK & STORKS:	BRAND-NEW KNOWLEDGE; LATEST DISCOVERY; FRESH SECRET
BOOK & DOG:	FRIEND'S SECRET; SUPPORTING KNOWLEDGE; ADVICE
BOOK & TOWER:	OFFICIAL SECRET; LEGAL KNOWLEDGE; ACADEMIA; RULES
BOOK & GARDEN:	PUBLIC KNOWLEDGE; CLASS; PUBLIC EDUCATION; LESSON
BOOK & MOUNTAIN:	BLOCKED EDUCATION; OBSTACLES TO DISCOVERY
BOOK & CROSSROAD:	MULTIPLE SOURCES OF INFO; MANY SECRETS; CHOICE OF KNOWLEDGE
BOOK & MICE	STRESSFUL SECRET; LEARNING ANXIETY; WORRYING INFORMATION
BOOK & HEART:	SECRET CRUSH; ROMANTIC SECRET; LOVE WISDOM
BOOK & RING:	MARRIAGE SECRETS; CONTRACT LAW; AGREEMENT INFORMATION
BOOK & LETTER:	MANUAL; NEWSPAPER; NEWS OF A SECRET; PUBLISHING
BOOK & MAN:	MAN'S KNOWLEDGE; MALE AUTHOR; MALE ACADEMIC
BOOK & WOMAN:	WOMAN'S KNOWLEDGE; FEMALE AUTHOR; FEMALE ACADEMIC
BOOK & LILY:	LONGSTANDING SECRET; WISDOM, LIFE EXPERIENCE
BOOK & SUN:	SECRET REVEALED; ACADEMIC SUCCESS; SUCCESSFUL BOOK
BOOK & MOON:	EMOTIONAL SECRET; NOVEL; INSTINCTIVE KNOWLEDGE
BOOK & KEY:	IMPORTANT SECRET; KEY INFORMATION; SIGNIFICANT KNOWLEDGE
BOOK & FISH:	BUSINESS LEARNING; BUSINESS SECRET; FREELANCE KNOWLEDGE
BOOK & ANCHOR:	ESTABLISHED KNOWLEDGE; NEVER-REVEALED SECRET; STABLE EDUCATION
BOOK & CROSS:	TROUBLING SECRET; WEIGHED DOWN BY KNOWLEDGE; WEIGHTY SECRET

27. LETTER

LETTER & RIDER:	NEWS ARRIVES, MESSAGE DELIVERY
LETTER & CLOVER:	FORTUNATE NEWS; LUCKY MESSAGE; WINNING TICKET
LETTER & SHIP:	NEWS FROM OVERSEAS; LETTER IN TRANSIT
LETTER & HOUSE:	DEEDS FOR A HOUSE; HOME DOCUMENTS; FAMILY NEWS
LETTER & TREE:	HEALTH LETTER; HEALTH CERTIFICATE; SPIRITUAL MESSAGE
LETTER & CLOUDS:	UNCLEAR DOCUMENTATION; CONFUSING NEWS
LETTER & SNAKE:	BAD NEWS; NEWS OF A BETRAYAL
LETTER & COFFIN:	FINAL LETTER; BEREAVEMENT NEWS; NEWS OF AN ENDING
LETTER & BOUQUET:	LOVELY MESSAGE; INVITATION; POSITIVE NEWS
LETTER & SCYTHE:	HURTFUL MESSAGE; NEWS OF DECISION; REDUNDANCY NEWS
LETTER & WHIP:	DIFFICULT NEWS; ABUSIVE MESSAGE; HARSH FEEDBACK
LETTER & BIRDS:	SOCIAL MEDIA MESSAGE; TEXT; CONVERSATIONAL LETTER
LETTER & CHILD:	CHILD'S MESSAGE; NEWS OF A CHILD; PREGNANCY NEWS
LETTER & FOX:	WORK DOCUMENTS; EMPLOYEE NEWS; DECEPTIVE MESSAGE
LETTER & BEAR:	FINANCIAL DOCUMENTS; FORCEFUL LETTER; MONEY NEWS
LETTER & STARS:	CELEBRITY PRESS; ACHIEVEMENT CERTIFICATE

LETTER & STORKS:	NEWS OF CHANGE; NEW START DOCUMENTATION
LETTER & DOG	FRIEND'S LETTER; NEWS OF FRIEND; WRITTEN SUPPORT
LETTER & TOWER:	OFFICIAL DOCUMENTS; PAPERS; CORPORATE NEWS
LETTER & GARDEN:	PUBLIC ANNOUNCEMENT; EVENT INVITATION
LETTER & MOUNTAIN:	DELAYED MESSAGE; NEWS BLOCKED; UNDELIVERED LETTER
LETTER & CROSSROAD:	MAILINGS; MULTI-PLATFORM INFO; MANY DOCUMENTS
LETTER & MICE:	WORRYING NEWS; ANXIOUS MESSAGE
LETTER & HEART:	LOVE LETTER; ROMANTIC MESSAGE; NEWS OF A ROMANCE
LETTER & RING:	CONTRACT; MARRIAGE CERTIFICATE; WRITTEN AGREEMENT
LETTER & BOOK:	EXAM CERTIFICATE; HIDDEN MESSAGE; ESSAY
LETTER & MAN:	MAN'S NEWS; MALE WRITER; MESSAGE FROM A MAN
LETTER & WOMAN:	WOMAN'S NEWS; FEMALE WRITER; MESSAGE FROM A WOMAN
LETTER & LILY:	MESSAGE FROM AN OLDER PERSON; WISE MESSAGE
LETTER & SUN:	NEWS OF SUCCESS; HAPPY NEWS; POSITIVE MESSAGE
LETTER & MOON:	CREATIVE WRITING; EMOTIONAL MESSAGE; POETRY
LETTER & KEY:	IMPORTANT MESSAGE; SIGNIFICANT NEWS
LETTER & FISH:	BUSINESS LETTER; BUSINESS EMAILS; BLOG
LETTER & ANCHOR:	LONG-TERM NEWS; AGREEMENT; SAVED DOCUMENTS
LETTER & CROSS:	DIFFICULT NEWS; PAINFUL MESSAGE; DEPRESSING NEWS

28. MAN

MAN & RIDER:	MALE VISITOR; A NEW LOVER ON THE SCENE
MAN & CLOVER:	LUCKY MAN; OPPORTUNISTIC INDIVIDUAL
MAN & SHIP:	TRAVELLER; FOREIGN MAN
MAN & HOUSE:	FAMILY MAN; LANDLORD
MAN & TREE:	HEALTHY MAN; SPIRITUAL INDIVIDUAL; SHAMAN
MAN & CLOUDS:	CONFUSED INDIVIDUAL; MISLEADING INDIVIDUAL
MAN & SNAKE	UNTRUSTWORTHY MAN; MAN BRINGS PROBLEMS
MAN & COFFIN	DEPRESSED MAN
MAN & BOUQUET:	HANDSOME MAN; CHARMING INDIVIDUAL; PLEASANT MAN
MAN & SCYTHE:	DECISIVE MAN; VIOLENT INDIVIDUAL ; ABRUPT PERSON
MAN & WHIP:	ABUSIVE MAN; SPORTSMAN; TRAINER; SEXUAL MAN
MAN & BIRDS:	TALKATIVE MAN; PRESS OFFICER; THERAPIST
MAN & CHILD:	CHILDISH MAN; BOY; IMMATURE INDIVIDUAL
MAN & FOX:	EMPLOYEE; CUNNING MAN; WHEELER-DEALER
MAN & BEAR:	PROTECTIVE MAN; MALE MANAGER; PROVIDER
MAN & STARS:	MALE CELEBRITY; HIGH-FLIER; ALPHA MALE; ASTRONAUT

MAN & STORKS:	PROGRESSIVE MAN; FLEXIBLE INDIVIDUAL
MAN & DOG:	MALE PARTNER; FRIENDLY MAN; MALE FRIEND
MAN & TOWER:	OFFICIAL; MALE LAWYER; TALL MAN; ARROGANT MAN
MAN & GARDEN:	SOCIABLE MAN; PUBLIC FIGURE; GROUP OF MEN
MAN & MOUNTAIN:	LONELY MAN; STUBBORN INDIVIDUAL; STICK-IN-THE-MUD
MAN & CROSSROAD:	COMMITMENT- PHOBE; MAN WITH CHOICES; SEVERAL MEN
MAN & MICE:	ANXIOUS MAN; STRESSED INDIVIDUAL
MAN & HEART:	LOVING MAN; LOVER; SOULMATE
MAN & RING:	HUSBAND; COMMITTED MAN; MARRIED MAN; LAWYER
MAN & BOOK:	AUTHOR; ACADEMIC; INTELLIGENT MAN; TEACHER
MAN & LETTER	WRITER; JOURNALIST; POSTMAN; BLOGGER
MAN & WOMAN:	COUPLE; MAN AND WOMAN
MAN & LILY:	FATHER; OLDER MAN; FATHER FIGURE; MENTOR
MAN & SUN:	SUCCESSFUL MAN; VICTOR; POSITIVE OR HAPPY MAN
MAN & MOON:	EMOTIONAL MAN; CREATIVE MAN
MAN & KEY:	SIGNIFICANT INDIVIDUAL; SOULMATE; IMPORTANT MAN
MAN & FISH:	BUSINESSMAN; FREELANCER; ENTREPRENEUR
MAN & ANCHOR:	SETTLED MAN; STABLE INDIVIDUAL; RELIABLE
MAN & CROSS	DEPRESSED MAN; PRIEST; SAINT

29. WOMAN

WOMAN & RIDER:	FEMALE VISITOR; A NEW FEMALE LOVER
WOMAN & CLOVER:	LUCKY WOMAN; OPPORTUNISTIC INDIVIDUAL
WOMAN & SHIP:	TRAVELLER; FOREIGN WOMAN
WOMAN & HOUSE:	FAMILY WOMAN; HOUSEKEEPER; HOMEMAKER; LANDLADY
WOMAN & TREE:	HEALTHY WOMAN; SPIRITUAL PERSON; HEALER
WOMAN & CLOUDS:	CONFUSED WOMAN; MISLEADING INDIVIDUAL
WOMAN & SNAKE:	UNTRUSTWORTHY WOMAN; TEMPTRESS
WOMAN & COFFIN:	DEPRESSED WOMAN
WOMAN & BOUQUET:	ATTRACTIVE WOMAN; CHARMING; NICE LADY
WOMAN & SCYTHE:	DECISIVE WOMAN; HARSH INDIVIDUAL; ABRUPT PERSON
WOMAN & WHIP:	TOUGH WOMAN; SPORTSWOMAN; TRAINER; DOMINATRIX
WOMAN & BIRDS:	CHATTY WOMAN; COMMUNICATOR; PRESS OFFICER;
WOMAN & CHILD:	CHILDISH WOMAN; GIRL; IMMATURE INDIVIDUAL
WOMAN & FOX:	EMPLOYEE; DECEITFUL WOMAN
WOMAN & BEAR:	PROTECTIVE WOMAN; BOSS; MOTHER; WEALTHY WOMAN
WOMAN & STARS:	FEMALE CELEB; HIGH-ACHIEVER; ALPHA FEMALE; ASTRONAUT

WOMAN & STORKS:	PROGRESSIVE WOMAN; FLEXIBLE INDIVIDUAL
WOMAN & DOG:	FEMALE PARTNER; FRIENDLY WOMAN; FEMALE FRIEND
WOMAN & TOWER:	OFFICIAL; FEMALE LAWYER; TALL WOMAN; QUEEN
WOMAN & GARDEN:	SOCIABLE WOMAN; PUBLIC FIGURE; GROUP OF WOMEN
WOMAN & MOUNTAIN:	LONELY WOMAN; STUBBORN INDIVIDUAL
WOMAN & CROSSROAD:	COMMITMENT-PHOBE; SEVERAL WOMEN; CHOOSY WOMAN
WOMAN & MICE:	ANXIOUS WOMAN; STRESSED INDIVIDUAL
WOMAN & HEART:	LOVING WOMAN; LOVER; SOULMATE
WOMAN & RING:	WIFE; COMMITTED WOMAN; MARRIED WOMAN
WOMAN & BOOK:	AUTHOR; ACADEMIC; INTELLIGENT WOMAN; TEACHER
WOMAN & LETTER:	WRITER; JOURNALIST; POSTWOMAN; BLOGGER
WOMAN & MAN:	COUPLE; WOMAN AND MAN
WOMAN & LILY:	OLDER WOMAN; GRANDMOTHER; MENTOR
WOMAN & SUN:	SUCCESSFUL WOMAN; WINNER; POSITIVE OR HAPPY WOMAN
WOMAN & MOON:	EMOTIONAL WOMAN; CREATIVE WOMAN
WOMAN & KEY:	SIGNIFICANT INDIVIDUAL; SOULMATE; IMPORTANT WOMAN
WOMAN & FISH:	BUSINESSWOMAN; FREELANCER; ENTREPRENEUR
WOMAN & ANCHOR:	SETTLED WOMAN; STABLE INDIVIDUAL; RELIABLE
WOMAN & CROSS:	DEPRESSED WOMAN; RELIGIOUS WOMAN; SAINT

30. LILY

LILY & RIDER:	MATURITY; ONSET OF OLD AGE; ARRIVAL OF OLDER PERSON
LILY & CLOVER:	LUCK COMES WITH WISDOM; LATER-LIFE GOOD FORTUNE;
LILY & SHIP:	TRAVELLING OLDER PERSON; FOREIGN SENIOR CITIZEN
LILY & HOUSE:	HEAD OF THE FAMILY; HOUSEBOUND OLDER PERSON
LILY & TREE:	OLD AGE HEALTH ISSUES; HEALTHY OLD AGE; SPIRITUAL PEACE
LILY & CLOUDS	CONFUSED SENIOR; DEMENTIA
LILY & SNAKE:	PROBLEMS OF OLD AGE; UNTRUSTWORTHY OLDER PERSON
LILY & COFFIN:	END OF LIFE ISSUES; END OF WISDOM
LILY & BOUQUET:	HAPPY OLD AGE; BLOOMING MATURITY; LATE BLOOMER
LILY & SCYTHE:	SURGERY FOR OLDER PERSON; DECISIVE OLDER PERSON
LILY & WHIP:	DIFFICULT SENIOR; TOUGH MENTOR; STRUGGLES OF OLD AGE
LILY & BIRDS:	OLDER COUPLE; VERBAL ADVICE; TALKATIVE SENIOR
LILY & CHILD:	YOUTHFUL OLDER PERSON; LATE STARTER; ELDEST CHILD
LILY & FOX:	WORK SENIORITY; WORK EXPERIENCE; WILY OLD FOX
LILY & BEAR:	POWERFUL ELDER; PROTECTIVE FATHER FIGURE
LILY & STARS:	ESTABLISHED STAR; HIGH-FLYING SENIOR

LILY & STORKS:	LATE STARTER; FRESH START FOR SENIOR
LILY & DOG:	LIFELONG FRIEND; FRIENDLY OLDER PERSON
LILY & TOWER:	ESTABLISHMENT; OLD ORDER; HIGH-RANKING OLDER PERSON
LILY & GARDEN:	PUBLIC PARK; GROUP OF SENIORS
LILY & MOUNTAIN:	ISOLATED OLDER PERSON; RIGID OLDER PERSON
LILY & CROSSROAD:	CHOICES OF OLD AGE; MATURE OPTIONS
LILY & MICE:	ANXIOUS SENIOR; STRESSFUL OLD AGE
LILY & HEART:	LOVING OLDER PERSON; LIFE-LONG LOVE; LIFE'S PASSION
LILY & RING:	LONG-TERM RELATIONSHIP; OLD BOND; MARRIED ELDER
LILY & BOOK:	WISE ELDER; LIFE'S KNOWLEDGE; LONG-HELD SECRET
LILY & LETTER:	NEWS OF AN OLDER PERSON
LILY & MAN:	OLDER MAN; MALE MATURITY
LILY & WOMAN:	OLDER WOMAN; FEMALE MATURITY
LILY & SUN:	LATER IN LIFE SUCCESS; HAPPY OLD AGE
LILY & MOON:	EMOTIONAL MATURITY; CREATIVE COMING-OF-AGE
LILY & KEY:	IMPORTANT OLDER PERSON; SIGNIFICANT WISDOM
LILY & FISH:	BUSINESS MATURITY; BUSINESS MENTOR
LILY & ANCHOR:	LONG AND STABLE LIFE; SECURE OLD AGE
LILY & CROSS:	TROUBLED OLD AGE; DIFFICULTY IN LATER YEARS

31. SUN

SUN & RIDER:	VICTORY; SUCCESS IS COMING
SUN & CLOVER:	VERY SUCCESSFUL; GREAT OUTCOME; UNEXPECTED SUCCESS
SUN & SHIP:	TRAVEL TO HOT COUNTRY; SUMMER HOLIDAY
SUN & HOUSE:	DOMESTIC HAPPINESS; FAMILY SUCCESS
SUN & TREE:	GOOD HEALTH; SPIRITUAL HAPPINESS
SUN & CLOUDS:	MARRED SUCCESS; UNCERTAIN VICTORY
SUN & SNAKE:	PROBLEMATIC SUCCESS; NOT AS GOOD AS IT LOOKED; ENVY
SUN & COFFIN:	END OF A SUCCESSFUL PERIOD; POSITIVITY ENDS
SUN & BOUQUET:	HAPPINESS AND JOY; CELEBRATION; AWARD
SUN & SCYTHE:	SUDDEN SUCCESS; HAPPINESS IS SHORT-LIVED
SUN & WHIP:	VICTORY; SUCCESS BRINGS STRAIN; CHALLENGING SUCCESS
SUN & BIRDS:	POSITIVE TALK; MEETING SUCCESS; GOOD CONVERSATION
SUN & CHILD:	CHILD'S HAPPINESS; CHILD'S ACHIEVEMENT; SMALL SUCCESS
SUN & FOX:	SUCCESS AT WORK; WORK HAPPINESS; CLEVERNESS
SUN & BEAR:	FINANCIAL SUCCESS; PROTECTIVE POSITIVITY
SUN & STARS:	BIG ACHIEVEMENT; FAME; HOPES OF SUCCESS; SHINING STAR

SUN & STORKS	POSITIVE NEW START; GOOD PROGRESS
SUN & DOG:	POSITIVE FRIENDSHIP; FRIEND'S HAPPINESS; FRIEND'S SUCCESS
SUN & TOWER	HIGH STATUS ACHIEVEMENT; ESTABLISHED SUCCESS
SUN & GARDEN:	GROUP ACHIEVEMENT; TEAM VICTORY; SOCIAL SUCCESS
SUN & MOUNTAIN:	OBSTACLES TO ACHIEVEMENT; BLOCKS TO HAPPINESS
SUN & CROSSROAD:	MULTIPLE ACHIEVEMENTS; POSITIVE CHOICE
SUN & MICE:	IMPOSTER SYNDROME; STRESSFUL ACHIEVEMENT
SUN & HEART:	LOVE AND HAPPINESS; ROMANTIC SUCCESS
SUN & RING:	HAPPY MARRIAGE; SUCCESSFUL PARTNERSHIP
SUN & BOOK:	SECRET JOY; UNKNOWN HAPPINESS; SUCCESSFUL EDUCATION
SUN & LETTER:	MESSAGE OF POSITIVITY; EMPOWERING MOTTO
SUN & MAN:	MAN'S ACHIEVEMENT; MAN'S SUCCESS; MAN'S HAPPINESS
SUN & WOMAN:	WOMAN'S ACHIEVEMENT; SUCCESS; WOMAN'S HAPPINESS
SUN & LILY:	LATE-IN-LIFE SUCCESS; HAPPINESS; HAPPY OLD AGE
SUN & MOON:	CREATIVE SUCCESS; EMOTIONAL POSITIVITY
SUN & KEY:	SIGNIFICANT ACHIEVEMENT; FATED SUCCESS
SUN & FISH:	BUSINESS SUCCESS; BUSINESS POSITIVITY
SUN & ANCHOR:	SETTLED AND HAPPY; LONG TERM SUCCESS
SUN & CROSS:	PRESSURED SUCCESS; WEIGHED DOWN BY ACHIEVEMENTS

32. MOON

MOON & RIDER:	PERIOD OF CREATIVITY; EMOTIONAL VISITOR; NEW ROMANCE
MOON & CLOVER:	LUCKY INSTINCT; POSITIVE FEELINGS; ROMANTIC HAPPINESS
MOON & SHIP	EMOTIONAL TRIP; UP-AND-DOWN FEELINGS; HONEYMOON
MOON & HOUSE:	HOMESICKNESS; EMOTIONS CONNECTED WITH HOME
MOON & TREE	PSYCHIC; BUDDING CREATIVITY; EMOTIONAL HEALTH
MOON & CLOUDS:	CONFUSED FEELINGS; MIXED EMOTIONS;
MOON & SNAKE:	BETRAYED; UNPLEASANT FEELINGS; SENSE OF DANGER
MOON & COFFIN:	DEPRESSION; EMOTIONAL BLANKNESS; SHOCK
MOON & BOUQUET:	LOVELY FEELINGS; JOY; HAPPY EMOTIONS; VISUAL ART
MOON & SCYTHE:	HURT FEELINGS; SUDDEN EMOTION; CUT OFF FEELINGS
MOON & WHIP:	DIFFICULT EMOTIONS; CHALLENGING FEELINGS
MOON & BIRDS:	TALKING ABOUT FEELINGS; THERAPY; CREATIVE TALK
MOON & CHILD:	CHILD'S EMOTIONS; KIDS' CREATIVITY; EARLY FEELINGS
MOON & FOX:	FEELINGS OF DISTRUST; WORK-RELATED EMOTIONS
MOON & BEAR	POWERFUL EMOTIONS; PROTECTIVE FEELING
MOON & STARS:	DREAMS; DRAMA; FAMOUS CREATIVITY OR ARTISTRY

MOON & STORKS:	EMOTIONAL NEW START; NEW FEELINGS
MOON & DOG:	FRIENDLY FEELINGS; PARTNER'S EMOTIONS; SOULMATE
MOON & TOWER:	TOP CREATIVITY; SNOBBY FEELINGS; EMOTIONAL ISOLATION
MOON & GARDEN:	GROUP EMOTIONS; PUBLIC DISPLAY OF EMOTION
MOON & MOUNTAIN:	BLOCKED FEELINGS; CREATIVE BLOCK
MOON & CROSSROAD:	CHOICE OF EMOTIONS; MANY DIFFERENT FEELINGS
MOON & MICE	ANXIOUS FEELINGS; HIGHLY-STRUNG; STRESS
MOON & HEART:	LOVING FEELINGS; PASSIONATE EMOTIONS
MOON & RING	CREATIVE CONTRACT; ART PAYMENT; LINKED EMOTIONS
MOON & BOOK:	SECRET FEELINGS; EMOTIONAL INTELLIGENCE; NOVEL
MOON & LETTER:	CREATIVE WRITING; POETRY; EMOTIONAL MESSAGE
MOON & MAN:	MALE EMOTIONS; MAN'S FEELINGS; MAN'S CREATIVITY
MOON & WOMAN:	FEMALE EMOTIONS; FEELINGS; WOMAN'S CREATIVITY
MOON & LILY:	MATURE EMOTIONS; FULLY-DEVELOPED CREATIVITY
MOON & SUN:	POSITIVE EMOTIONS; HAPPY ROMANCE; CREATIVE SUCCESS
MOON & KEY:	SIGNIFICANT FEELINGS; IMPORTANT SIGN; GUT FEELING
MOON & FISH:	BUSINESS SENSE; CREATIVE BUSINESS; FEELINGS OF FREEDOM
MOON & ANCHOR:	STABLE EMOTIONS; LONG TERM FEELINGS
MOON & CROSS:	DEPRESSION; HEAVY FEELINGS; EMOTIONAL BURDENS

33. KEY

KEY & RIDER:	KEY EVENT; IMPORTANT VISITOR; SOMETHING BIG COMING
KEY & CLOVER:	FATED LUCK; LUCKY KARMA; SIGNIFICANT GOOD FORTUNE
KEY & SHIP:	IMPORTANT JOURNEY; TRIP OF A LIFETIME; DESTINY;
KEY & HOUSE:	HOUSE KEY; TRUE NORTH; IMPORTANT HOUSE
KEY & TREE:	SPIRITUAL SIGNIFICANCE; KARMIC FORCES; HEALTH ANSWER
KEY & CLOUDS:	UNCERTAIN FATE; ANSWER UNCLEAR; HIDDEN SIGNIFICANCE
KEY & SNAKE:	ILL-FATED; NEGATIVE ANSWER; LIES; BAD KARMA; DANGER
KEY & COFFIN:	IMPORTANT ENDING; FINAL ANSWER; BIG LIFE CHANGE
KEY & BOUQUET:	SIGNIFICANT GIFT; POSITIVE DESTINY; BLESSED;
KEY & SCYTHE	IMPORTANT DECISION; TURNING POINT; FATED DECISION
KEY & WHIP:	BIG ARGUMENT; KEY CONFLICT; FATED CHALLENGE;
KEY & BIRDS:	IMPORTANT CONVERSATION; NECESSARY COMMUNICATION
KEY & CHILD:	SIGNIFICANT CHILD; IMPORTANT BEGINNINGS
KEY & FOX:	JOB IMPORTANCE; DEEPLY UNTRUSTWORTHY
KEY & BEAR:	FINANCIAL KEY; PROTECTIVE KARMA; POWERFUL DESTINY
KEY & STARS:	DESTINED TO BE KNOWN; GOALS WILL BE ACHIEVED

KEY & STORKS:	FRESH START NEEDED; FATED NEW BEGINNING
KEY & DOG:	SIGNIFICANT FRIEND; SOULMATE; FATED COMPANION
KEY & TOWER:	OFFICIAL IMPORTANCE; AT THE HIGHEST LEVEL
KEY & GARDEN:	PUBLIC SIGNIFICANCE; SHARED ANSWER; IMPORTANT EVENT
KEY & MOUNTAIN:	SIGNIFICANT OBSTACLE; FATED DELAY
KEY & CROSSROAD:	SIGNIFICANT LIFE CHOICES; CHOOSE WELL
KEY & MICE:	SIGNIFICANT CONCERNS; IMPORTANT WORRIES
KEY & HEART:	ROMANTIC FATE; LOVE DESTINY; SIGNIFICANT ROMANCE
KEY & RING:	IMPORTANT CONTRACT; FATED LINK; KEY RELATIONSHIP
KEY & BOOK:	THE ANSWER; FORTUNE TELLING; SIGNIFICANT KNOWLEDGE
KEY & LETTER:	WRITTEN ANSWER; IMPORTANT MESSAGE
KEY & MAN:	SIGNIFICANT MAN; SOULMATE; MAN'S DESTINY
KEY & WOMAN:	SIGNIFICANT WOMAN; SOULMATE; WOMAN'S DESTINY
KEY & LILY:	EXPERIENCE KEY; IMPORTANT OLDER PERSON; MENTOR
KEY & SUN:	BIG SUCCESS; HUGE ACHIEVEMENT; SUCCESS IS ASSURED
KEY & MOON:	CORE FEELINGS; SENSE OF SIGNIFICANCE; PSYCHIC FEELINGS
KEY & FISH:	BUSINESS FATE; KEY TO THE BUSINESS
KEY & ANCHOR:	LONG-TERM FATE; DESTINY; THE ONLY ANSWER
KEY & CROSS:	RELIGIOUS CONVERSION; TROUBLED FATE; GUILT

34. FISH

FISH & RIDER:	BUSINESS ARRIVAL ON THE SCENE; BUSINESS NEWS
FISH & CLOVER:	LUCKY BUSINESS; BUSINESS OPPORTUNITY; GOOD FORTUNE
FISH & SHIP:	OVERSEAS BUSINESS; TRAVEL BUSINESS; TRADE
FISH & HOUSE:	WORKING FROM HOME; DOMESTIC BUSINESS; FAMILY WORK
FISH & TREE:	HEALTH SERVICES; SPIRITUAL BUSINESS; GROWING BUSINESS
FISH & CLOUDS:	UNCLEAR BUSINESS; UNCERTAIN WORK
FISH & SNAKE	DODGY BUSINESS; UNTRUSTWORTHY, SLIPPERY.
FISH & COFFIN:	UNDERTAKERS; FUNERAL BUSINESS; BUSINESS ENDING
FISH & BOUQUET:	BEAUTY BUSINESS; FLORIST; PLEASANT BUSINESS
FISH & SCYTHE:	BUSINESS CUTS; DENTIST; BUSINESS DECISIONS
FISH & WHIP:	COACHING, TRAINING WORK; SPORTS BUSINESS
FISH & BIRDS:	PRESS OFFICE; COMMS BUSINESS; VOICEOVER WORK
FISH & CHILD:	WORKING WITH CHILDREN; NANNY
FISH & FOX:	CORPORATE WORK; EMPLOYED; UNDERHAND BUSINESS
FISH & BEAR:	FINANCIAL BUSINESS; BODYBUILDING; FOOD INDUSTRY
FISH & STARS:	AGENT; CELEBRITY WORK; AMBITIOUS BUSINESS

FISH & STORKS:	NEW BUSINESS; BUSINESS CHANGES; STARTUP
FISH & DOG:	BUSINESS PARTNERSHIP; WORKING WITH SOMEONE YOU KNOW
FISH & TOWER:	OFFICIAL BUSINESS; CORPORATE CONTRACTOR; LEGAL WORK
FISH & GARDEN:	PUBLIC WORK; PUBLIC RELATIONS; PARTY PLANNER
FISH & MOUNTAIN:	BLOCKED BUSINESS; FREEDOM CURTAILED
FISH & CROSSROAD:	MULTIPLE BUSINESSES; CHOICE OF WORK; CHOICE OF BUSINESS
FISH & MICE:	STRESSFUL WORK; BUSINESS WORRIES
FISH & HEART:	PASSIONATE JOB; DATING AGENCY
FISH & RING:	WORKING ON CONTRACTS; BUSINESS PARTNERSHIP; MERGER
FISH & BOOK:	PUBLISHING; ACADEMIC WORK
FISH & LETTER	FREELANCE WRITING; JOURNALISM
FISH & MAN:	BUSINESSMAN; MAN'S BUSINESS; BUSINESS FOR MALES
FISH & WOMAN:	BUSINESSWOMAN; WOMAN'S BUSINESS; BUSINESS FOR WOMEN
FISH & LILY:	MATURE BUSINESS; WORK WITH OLDER PEOPLE; CONSULTANT
FISH & SUN:	SUCCESSFUL BUSINESS; ESCAPE
FISH & MOON:	CREATIVE WORK; EMOTION-RELATED BUSINESS
FISH & KEY:	SIGNIFICANT BUSINESS; IMPORTANT CAREER
FISH & ANCHOR:	LONG-TERM BUSINESS; STABLE BUSINESS; LONG-TERM FREEDOM
FISH & CROSS:	COUNSELLING WORK; SPIRITUAL WORKER; THERAPIST

35. ANCHOR

ANCHOR & RIDER:	STABILITY ARRIVES; A SENSE OF PERMANENCE
ANCHOR & CLOVER:	CERTAIN GOOD FORTUNE; LASTING LUCK
ANCHOR & SHIP:	LONG JOURNEY; HARBOUR; MOORED
ANCHOR & HOUSE:	DOMESTIC STABILITY; PERMANENT HOME; STABLE FAMILY
ANCHOR & TREE:	LONG-TERM HEALTH; LONGEVITY; SPIRITUAL CORE
ANCHOR & CLOUDS:	UNSETTLED; UNCLEAR WHAT IS NEEDED; UPROOTED
ANCHOR & SNAKE:	LONG-TERM PROBLEMS; DANGER
ANCHOR & COFFIN:	STABILITY ENDS; FINALITY
ANCHOR & BOUQUET:	CONTENTMENT; HAPPILY SETTLED; COMFORTABLE
ANCHOR & SCYTHE:	SUDDEN CHANGES; RUG PULLED FROM UNDER YOUR FEET
ANCHOR & WHIP:	LONG-TERM HARDSHIP; ADDICTION; CONSTANT STRUGGLE
ANCHOR & BIRDS:	LONG CONVERSATION; LIFELONG COMPANION
ANCHOR & CHILD:	FOREVER CHILDLIKE; STUBBORNNESS
ANCHOR & FOX:	WORK STABILITY; PERMANENT JOB
ANCHOR & BEAR:	FINANCIAL STABILITY; PROTECTION AND SAFETY
ANCHOR & STARS:	LONG-TERM AMBITIONS; ACHIEVING GOALS

ANCHOR & STORKS:	STABLE NEW START; PERMANENT CHANGE
ANCHOR & DOG:	LOYALTY; STEADFASTNESS; LONG-TERM FRIENDSHIP
ANCHOR & TOWER:	RIGIDITY; IMPERIOUSNESS; PRISON
ANCHOR & GARDEN:	GROUP STABILITY; LONG-TERM NETWORK
ANCHOR & MOUNTAIN	STAGNATION; STUCK OR BLOCKED FROM MOVING ON
ANCHOR & CROSSROAD:	UNCOMMITTED; KEEPING OPTIONS OPEN
ANCHOR & MICE:	CLINGINESS; DEPENDENCE; ANXIOUS ATTACHMENT
ANCHOR & HEART:	STABLE ROMANCE; LONG-TERM LOVE
ANCHOR & RING:	COMMITMENT; STABLE MARRIAGE; LONG-TERM PARTNERSHIP
ANCHOR & BOOK:	STALLED LEARNING; STUCK IN THEIR WAYS
ANCHOR & LETTER:	WRITTEN COMMITMENT; SIGNATURE
ANCHOR & MAN:	RELIABLE MAN; STUBBORN MAN
ANCHOR & WOMAN:	RELIABLE WOMAN; STUBBORN WOMAN
ANCHOR & LILY:	VINTAGE; ROOTS; LIFELONG STABILITY
ANCHOR & SUN:	LONG-TERM HAPPINESS; STABLE SUCCESS
ANCHOR & MOON:	EMOTIONAL STABILITY; CREATIVE HUB
ANCHOR & KEY:	LONG-TERM SUCCESS; IMPORTANT STABILITY
ANCHOR & FISH:	BUSINESS STABILITY; LONGSTANDING BUSINESS
ANCHOR & CROSS:	LONG-TERM TROUBLES; WEIGHTY ISSUES

36. CROSS

Cross & Rider: HARD TIME AHEAD; RELIGIOUS REVIVAL; PRESSURE COMING

Cross & Clover: PROBLEMS RESOLVE; TROUBLES BRING LUCK

Cross & Ship: PROBLEMS ON A JOURNEY; TROUBLED TRIP; OVERSEAS ISSUES

Cross & House: FAMILY TROUBLES; DOMESTIC ISSUES; HOUSE PROBLEMS

Cross & Tree   HEALTH PROBLEMS; SPIRITUAL CRISIS

Cross & Clouds: MENTAL HEALTH ISSUES; DEMENTIA; SERIOUS CONFUSION

Cross & Snake: SERIOUS DIFFICULTIES; UPSET OVER BETRAYAL; CRISIS

Cross & Coffin: FUNERAL; THE END OF TROUBLES

Cross & Bouquet: BEAUTY ISSUES; TROUBLED APPEARANCE; LIGHT BURDENS

Cross & Scythe: ACCIDENT; HARD DECISION; PROBLEMS SWIFTLY RESOLVE

Cross & Whip: ABUSE; VIOLENCE; OVER-PRESSURED; SEXUAL DIFFICULTIES

Cross & Birds: DIFFICULT COMMUNICATION; HEAVY TALK; VERBAL PRESSURE

Cross & Child: HEAVILY PREGNANT; KID PROBLEMS; TROUBLED YOUNGSTER

Cross & Fox: SEVERE PRESSURE AT WORK; UNDERHANDED PROBLEM

Cross & Bear   FINANCIAL DIFFICULTIES; HEAVY RESPONSIBILITY

Cross & Stars: THE PROBLEMS OF FAME; ACHIEVEMENT BRINGS DIFFICULTIES

CROSS & STORKS:	DIFFICULT NEW START; FRESH BEGINNINGS AFTER HARDSHIP
CROSS & DOG:	COUNSELLING, MORAL SUPPORT; HELPING OUT
CROSS & TOWER:	PROBLEMS WITH OFFICIALS; RELIGIOUS BURDENS; GUILT
CROSS & GARDEN:	PUBLIC PRESSURE; SHARED TROUBLES; SUPPORT GROUP
CROSS & MOUNTAIN:	PROBLEMS PREVENTED; DEPRESSION & ISOLATION; DELAYS
CROSS & CROSSROAD:	MULTIPLE BURDENS; NO EASY CHOICES
CROSS & MICE	SERIOUS STRESS, DEPRESSION, ANXIETY; UNDER PRESSURE
CROSS & HEART:	ROMANTIC TROUBLES; DIFFICULT LOVE LIFE
CROSS & RING	RESTRICTIVE RELATIONSHIP; BURDENSOME PARTNERSHIP;
CROSS & BOOK:	LEARNING DIFFICULTIES; SECRET TROUBLES; BIBLE
CROSS & LETTER:	UPSETTING NEWS; RELIGIOUS WRITINGS
CROSS & MAN:	MAN'S TROUBLES; STRESSED MAN; MARTYR
CROSS & WOMAN:	WOMAN'S TROUBLES; STRESSED WOMAN; MARTYR
CROSS & LILY:	THE PROBLEMS OF OLD AGE; WEIGHED DOWN BY EXPERIENCE
CROSS & SUN:	SUCCESS AFTER A TROUBLED TIME; EVENTUAL HAPPINESS
CROSS & MOON:	EMOTIONALLY TROUBLED; CREATIVE DIFFICULTIES
CROSS & KEY:	SPIRITUAL CRISIS; FUTURE TROUBLES
CROSS & FISH	BUSINESS TROUBLES; CASHFLOW ISSUES
CROSS & ANCHOR:	LONG TERM DIFFICULTIES; DEPRESSION; HEAVY BURDEN

Card Meaning & Combo Exercises

Use the Exercises in this section to help test your knowledge and understanding of the cards. It's best to try and fill them in yourself if you can without referring back to the lists. The aim of them is to help build your confidence and independence in reading the cards, and help prise you from reliance on combination lists!

Exercises 1-4 check your understanding of the cards and their meanings

Exercise 5 gets you listing as many of the **nouns** and **adjectives** for random card combinations as you can and then making your own meanings out of them.

Exercise 6 gives some sample card combinations. I urge you to try to come up with them yourself first WITHOUT referring back to the Combination Lists but by using the Noun + Adjective method

Exercise 7 is a tricky but useful exercise and encourages you to 'reverse-think' the cards. Please note with this one, there is often more than one possible answer, and you'll find yourself needing to think creatively and laterally.

Answers are provided at the end.

EXERCISES

Exercise 1:

Which cards might you associate with the following?

Beauty   _____

Burden   _____

Change   _____

Choices   _____

Confusion   _____

Contract   _____

Creativity   _____

Depression   _____

Decision   _____

Document   _____

Enterprise   _____

Fame   _____

Family   _____

Friend   _____

Government   _____

KNOWLEDGE	_____
LOVE	_____
LUCK	_____
OBSTACLE	_____
OLD PERSON	_____
PUBLIC	_____
SPEECH	_____
STABILITY	_____
SUCCESS	_____
TRAVEL	_____
TROUBLE	_____
VISITOR	_____

EXERCISE 2

AND THE FOLLOWING?

YOUNG	_____
WRITTEN	_____
WORRIED	_____
VERBAL	_____
UPCOMING	_____
SUCCESSFUL	_____

Social _____

Significant _____

Protective _____

Official _____

Negative _____

Married _____

Lovely _____

Harsh _____

Healthy _____

Fresh _____

Fortunate _____

Financial _____

Feminine _____

Experienced _____

Emotional _____

Educational _____

Domestic _____

Delayed _____

Corporate _____

Confusing _____

Ambitious _____

Exercise 3

WHICH NOUNS - THINGS, PEOPLE - MIGHT YOU LINK WITH THE FOLLOWING CARDS?

Snake _____

Lily _____

Child _____

Scythe _____

Bouquet _____

Tree _____

Heart _____

Key _____

Fox _____

Mice _____

Book _____

Cross _____

Ship _____

Moon _____

Fish _____

Clover _____

Rider _____

Anchor _____

Tower _____

House _____

Bear _____

Ring _____

Fish _____

Mountain _____

Garden _____

Birds _____

Letter _____

Exercise 4

Which adjectives might you link with these cards?

Fish _____

Whip _____

Clouds _____

Crossroads _____

Storks _____

Scythe _____

Coffin _____

Bouquet _____

Tower _____

STARS _____
BOOK _____
HOUSE _____
GARDEN _____
DOG _____
SHIP _____
SUN _____
TREE _____
MOUNTAIN _____
CROSS _____
HEART _____
RING _____
BIRDS _____
LILY _____
MOON _____
RIDER _____
ANCHOR _____
FOX _____

Exercise 5

This exercise forces you to start thinking actively about the card meanings and combinations for yourself.

- Take a sheet of paper and divide it down the middle into two columns

- Take **TWO** cards randomly from your Lenormand deck. Any two cards.

- Write the name of the **first card** at the top of **Column 1,** and the name of the **second card** at the top of **Column 2**

Example

Column 1   Column 2

SCYTHE   MOUNTAIN

- Now (and you may want to set yourself a time limit, say a minute), in Column 1, list as many nouns - things, people, ideas, places - you can *possibly* think of that represent the card at the top of that column. Try to get as many down as you can. Some examples for the Scythe card: *decision, cut, accident, harm, hurt, pain* etc

- Next, in Column 2, list all the adjectives - describing words - you can think of that represent the card at the top of *that* column. No nouns. *Only* adjectives. Give yourself a minute or so, again and try to get as many as you possibly can. Examples for the Mountain: *blocked, delayed, stopped, prevented, put off.*

You should now have two lists - nouns down the left, adjectives on the right.

- Now, one by one, try to combine *every* single word from your right-hand column with every one of those on the left to create words and phrases that makes some sort of sense.

Some examples from the cards above:

A *blocked decision, an accident prevented, decision put off, putting off the pain.*

Exercise 6

What could these combinations mean?

Fox + Scythe   _____ _____

Heart + Anchor   _____

Fish + Sun   _____

Man + Bouquet   _____

Bouquet + Scythe_____

Bear + Clover   _____

Tree + Snake   _____

Tower + Key   _____

Book + Woman   _____

Moon + Ship   _____

Exercise 7

Which pairs of cards could represent these?

A Wedding   _____

Tough decision   _____

Health concerns   _____

Arguments   _____

A new job   _____

Secret affair   _____

C.e.o.   _____

Therapy   _____

Financial news   _____

Audience   _____

Sexy man   _____

Travel problems   _____

Rival business   _____

Great happiness   _____

97

ANSWERS

Exercise 1

Beauty	Bouquet
Burden	Cross
Change	Storks
Choices	Crossroads
Confusion	Clouds
Contract	Ring
Creativity	Moon
Depression	Coffin, Cross
Decision	Scythe
Document	Letter
Enterprise	Fish
Fame	Stars
Family	House
Friend	Dog
Government	Tower
Knowledge	Book
Love	Heart
Luck	Clover
Obstacle	Mountain
Old person	Lily
Public	Garden
Speech	Birds

STABILITY	ANCHOR
SUCCESS	SUN
TRAVEL	SHIP
TROUBLE	SNAKE, CROSS
VISITOR	RIDER

EXERCISE 2

YOUNG :	CHILD
WRITTEN:	LETTER
WORRIED:	MICE
VERBAL:	BIRDS
UPCOMING :	RIDER
SUCCESSFUL:	SUN
SOCIAL:	GARDEN
SIGNIFICANT:	KEY
PROTECTIVE:	BEAR
OFFICIAL:	TOWER
NEGATIVE:	SNAKE
MARRIED:	RING
LOVELY:	BOUQUET
HARSH:	WHIP
HEALTHY:	TREE
FRESH:	STORKS
FORTUNATE:	CLOVER
FINANCIAL:	BEAR, FISH
FEMININE:	WOMAN
EXPERIENCED:	LILY
EMOTIONAL:	MOON

EDUCATIONAL:	BOOK
DOMESTIC:	HOUSE
DELAYED:	MOUNTAIN
CORPORATE:	TOWER
CONFUSING:	CLOUDS
AMBITIOUS	STARS

EXERCISE 3

SNAKE	SNAKE, BETRAYAL, PROBLEM, BAD GUY, CHEAT, OTHER WOMAN
LILY	PEACE, ELDER, SENIOR, OLDER PERSON, WISDOM
CHILD	CHILD, IMMATURE PERSON, NEWBIE, BEGINNER
SCYTHE	KNIFE, CUT, DECISION, ACCIDENT
BOUQUET	FLOWERS, BLOSSOM, BEAUTY, GIFT, BLESSING, DELIGHT, PLEASURE
TREE	TREE, HEALTH, SPIRITUALITY, WELLNESS, GROWTH, LIFE FORCE
HEART	HEART, LOVE, CARE PASSION, WARMTH
KEY	KEY, IMPORTANCE, SIGNIFICANCE, FATE
FOX	SURVIVOR, WORKER, DECEIT, THEFT, CUNNING
MICE	WORRY, NERVES, ANXIETY, JITTERS, NIGGLES
BOOK	BOOK, SCHOOL, EDUCATION, KNOWLEDGE, LEARNING, SECRET
CROSS	BURDEN, TROUBLES, DEPRESSION, RELIGION, DOGMA
SHIP	SHIP, TRAVEL, TRANSPORT, JOURNEY, MOVEMENT, TRANSFER
MOON	EMOTION, FEELING, CREATIVITY, PSYCHIC ABILITY, MOOD
FISH	BUSINESS, FREEDOM, INDEPENDENCE, CASHFLOW
CLOVER	LUCK, CHANCE, OPPORTUNITY, GOOD FORTUNE
RIDER	ARRIVAL, DELIVERY, NEWS, SOMEONE PASSING THROUGH, NEW PERSON
ANCHOR	STABILITY, SECURITY, FIXEDNESS
TOWER	BUILDING, CORPORATION, PRISON, GOVERNMENT, OFFICIALDOM

HOUSE	HOME, NAME, FAMILY, HOUSE
BEAR	MONEY, PROTECTION, POWER, WEIGHT
RING	RELATIONSHIP, CONNECTION, AGREEMENT, CONTRACT, BOND, MARRIAGE
FISH	BUSINESS, CASH-FLOW, FREEDOM, INDEPENDENCE, ENTREPRENEUR
MOUNTAIN	BLOCK, DELAY, OBSTACLE, CHALLENGE
GARDEN	GARDEN, PUBLIC, MARKETPLACE, NETWORK, GROUP
BIRDS	BIRDS, CHATTERBOX, CONVERSATION, COMMUNICATION, DISCUSSION
LETTER	LETTER, DOCUMENT, WRITTEN COMMUNICATION, NEWS

EXERCISE 4

FISH	FREE, BUSINESS-RELATED, INDEPENDENT, ENTREPRENEURIAL
WHIP	ABUSIVE, TOUGH, HARSH, SEXUAL, SPORTS-RELATED, TRAINING
CLOUDS	CONFUSING, UNCLEAR, BLURRED, CONFUSED
CROSSROADS	MULTIPLE, OPTIONAL, MANY, CHOICE-RELATED
STORKS	NEW, FRESH, RESTARTING, NEWLY BEGUN, STARTED
SCYTHE	DECISIVE, ACCIDENTAL, REDUCING, CUTTING, CUT, HURT, PAINFUL
COFFIN	FINAL, ENDING, DYING, DEAD, DEPRESSING, OVER
BOUQUET	BEAUTIFUL, LOVELY, PLEASANT, BLOSSOMING, BLOOMING, HAPPY
TOWER	OFFICIAL, HIGH-STATUS, SUPERIOR, LEGAL, CORPORATE
STARS	FAMOUS, HOPEFUL, AMBITIOUS, HIGH-ACHIEVING, ACCLAIMED
BOOK	BOOK-RELATED, EDUCATIONAL, LEARNING, SECRET, HIDDEN
HOUSE	DOMESTIC, HOUSE-RELATED, FAMILY-RELATED
GARDEN	PUBLIC, SHARED, GROUP, SOCIAL, SOCIABLE, OPEN
DOG	FRIENDLY, LOYAL, SUPPORTIVE, FAITHFUL
SHIP	TRAVELLING, TRANSPORT-RELATED, MOVING, TRANSFERRING
SUN	SUCCESSFUL, HAPPY, POSITIVE
TREE	HEALTHY, WELL, HEALTH-RELATED, SPIRITUAL, GROWING

MOUNTAIN	BLOCKED, DELAYED ISOLATED, LONELY
CROSS	HEAVY, WEIGHTY, BURDENED, PRESSURED, RELIGIOUS, GUILTY
HEART	LOVING, ROMANTIC, CARING, WARM
RING	AGREED, CONTRACTED, MARRIED, BOUND, BONDED, LINKED
BIRDS	VERBAL, SPOKEN, COMMUNICATIVE, CHATTY, CONVERSATIONAL
LILY	OLD, EXPERIENCED, WISE, PEACEFUL, ELDER, ELDEST, OLDER
MOON	EMOTIONAL, CREATIVE, MOODY, PSYCHIC, EMOTIVE
RIDER	ARRIVING, VISITING, UPCOMING, NEW
ANCHOR	STABLE, LONGTERM, SOLID, GROUNDED
FOX	WORK-RELATED, WORKING, DECEITFUL, CUNNING, WILY

EXERCISE 5

I hope you found this exercise useful and illuminating.

With luck, forcing yourself to think about the card meanings and combinations in this way will have got you thinking more laterally about the possible meanings of the card combinations you uncovered. You can think of Lenormand card combinations as a sort of code - and yourself as a great explorer unlocking the answers!

EXERCISE 6

The below answers aren't definitive, but hopefully, after the previous exercise, the answers you've come up with should be broadly on the right track.

FOX + SCYTHE	JOB LOSS, REDUNDANCY
HEART + ANCHOR	LONG-TERM ROMANCE, STABLE RELATIONSHIP, LASTING LOVE

FISH + SUN	SUCCESSFUL BUSINESS, ESCAPE, POSITIVE FREEDOM, BEACH HOLIDAY
MAN + BOUQUET	HANDSOME MAN; AGREEABLE MAN; LOVELY GUY
BOUQUET + SCYTHE	REDUCED PLEASURE, SUDDEN GIFT, BRIEF HAPPINESS
BEAR + CLOVER	WIN, LUCKY PROTECTION; FORTUNATE POWER
TREE + SNAKE	HEALTH PROBLEM; FAILING HEALTH, NEGATIVE KARMA
TOWER + KEY	IMPORTANT ORGANISATION; SIGNIFICANT STATUS
BOOK + WOMAN	WOMAN'S SECRET; FEMALE KNOWLEDGE; GIRLS' EDUCATION
MOON + SHIP	PROGRESSING CREATIVITY; EMOTIONAL JOURNEY; UPS & DOWN

EXERCISE 7

Again, these aren't necessarily definitive - what I hope you've got from this exercise, though, is the understanding of some of the nuances of the cards, and that the context in which you're reading them - and for whom - is incredibly important

A WEDDING	GARDEN + RING, RING+BOUQUET, GARDEN+HEART
TOUGH DECISION	CROSSROAD + WHIP, SCYTHE + WHIP, CROSS+SCYTHE
HEALTH CONCERNS	MICE+TREE, TREE+CROSS, CROSS + TREE
ARGUMENTS	BIRDS+WHIP, WHIP+HOUSE
A NEW JOB	FOX+STORKS, FOX+RIDER
SECRET AFFAIR	HEART+BOOK, HEART+SNAKE, WHIP+BOOK
C.E.O.	WOMAN/MAN+TOWER, WOMAN/MAN+STAR, BEAR+STAR, BEAR+TOWER,
THERAPY	DOG+BIRDS, DOG+CROSS, DOG+TREE
FINANCIAL NEWS	RIDER+BEAR, LETTER+BEAR, LETTER+FISH, RIDER+FISH
AUDIENCE	GARDEN+MOON, GARDEN+STAR

SEXY MAN	MAN+WHIP, MAN+BOUQUET
TRAVEL PROBLEMS	SHIP+SNAKE, SHIP+MOUNTAIN
A RIVAL BUSINESS	FISH+FOX, TOWER+FOX, FOX+FISH
GREAT HAPPINESS	BOUQUET+SUN, SUN+CLOVER, BOUQUET+CLOVER

FINALLY!

Thank you so much for reading this guide. I hope you've found the basic information and exercises provided here about Lenormand card meanings and combinations useful, and now feel more able to apply it to your own readings.

Do join me on the Lozzy's Lenormand website - **www.lozzyslenormand.com** - where you'll find further guidance and details on card layouts and readings, Lenormand decks, weekly readings, predictions, and much, much more!

Look forward to seeing you there!

All best, and happy Lenormand-reading!

Lozzy Phillips

About The Author

Lozzy Phillips is a freelance card reader, writer and author from the UK, who spent many years working in both teaching and corporate publishing before striking out on her own. She has lived and travelled all over the world—notably South America, and both Central and Western Europe—but is now settled back in her home country. She loves reading, cooking, writing fiction, current affairs - and earth-witchery in all its forms.

OTHER BOOKS BY THIS AUTHOR

Lozzy's Complete Guide To Lenormand. Ever want **all** the basics of Lenormand Card reading in one place? In this 200+ page highly practical reference guide & workbook, Lozzy Phillips guides the reader, step by step, through the fundamentals of the Lenormand system. Including:

- Detailed Card Meaning & Card Combination lists

- Step by step illustrated guide to all main Lenormand layouts: 3-Card, 5-Card, 9-Card, & The Grand Tableau, with example readings.

- Practical advice on working with Lenormand day-to-day

- Exercises & Practice Readings to test any aspiring Lenormand reader's knowledge!

- Links to downloadable worksheets & reference materials

Available as a paperback from Amazon & ebook from Kindle & all other ebook platforms

Lenormand Career & Work Readings. Being able to apply Lenormand Card meanings to particular contexts is a key skill of any aspiring Lenormand card reader. In this practical reference guide and workbook, Lenormand reader Lozzy Phillips places the focus on Lenormand card meanings for **Career & Work** contexts, as well as recapping basic Lenormand card meanings and step-by-step layouts. In addition, she provides several useful card meaning exercises, plus fourteen 3-Card, 5-Card & 9-Card practice Career readings to help readers practice their skills and & check their Lenormand knowledge.

Available as a paperback from Amazon & ebook from Kindle & all other ebook platforms.

Lenormand Love & Relationship Readings. Understanding Lenormand card meanings and being able to apply them to particular contexts is a key skill of any aspiring Lenormand card reader. In this highly practical reference guide and workbook, Lozzy Phillips places the focus on Lenormand card meanings for **Love & Relationship** contexts, as well as recapping basic Lenormand card meanings and step-by-step layouts. In addition, she provides several useful card meaning exercises, plus 3-Card, 5-Card & 9-Card practice Love & Relationship readings to help readers practice their skills and & check their Lenormand knowledge.

Available as a paperback from Amazon & ebook from Kindle & all other ebook platforms.

Made in the USA
Monee, IL
18 July 2021